# SYSTEMA
# HOLDS, LOCKS & THROWS

Robert Poyton

Copyright@ 2020  R Poyton

All rights reserved

The moral right of the author has been asserted

No part of this book may be reproduced in any form or by any electronic or mechanical means including information storage and retrieval systems, without permission in writing from the author. The only exception is by a reviewer, who may quote short excerpts in a review.

The author and publisher take no responsibility for any illness or injury resulting from practicing the exercises described in this book. Always consult your Doctor prior to training or if you have any medical issues.

Published by Cutting Edge

ISBN:978-1-64921-503-1

## ABOUT THE AUTHOR

Robert was born in the early 1960's in East London.
He trained in Judo and boxing as a child and at age
18 began training in Yang Family Taijiquan.

For many years he studied the Chinese Internal Arts in depth.
In the 1990's he set up his own school and began cross
training in several styles.

Robert has trained extensively with with Mikhail Ryabko and Vladimir
Vasiliev in both Moscow and Toronto. In addition he has arranged
numerous UK seminars for Mikhail, Vladimir and other instructors.

Robert now trains solely in Systema and runs regular classes
in the UK and teaches seminars throughout the UK and Europe.
He has been featured in numerous martial arts books and magazines
as well as producing his own publications and training films.

Outside of training, Robert is a professional musician and currently
lives in rural Bedfordshire with his wife and a small menagerie.

*"Rob Poyton has been training and teaching Systema since 2000.
He is a dedicated and talented instructor, knowledgeable on
all of the key components of Systema.
Rob presents his teaching in a clear and structured manner
through his classes and reading materials."*
- Vladimir Vasiliev, October 2019.

*"Comfort yields complacency.
Break free."*

— A.D. Posey

# CONTENTS

**CHAPTER 1: INTRODUCTION**
The Systema Approach ..... 10
How To Use This Book ..... 12

**CHAPTER 2: MECHANICS**
Simple Machines ..... 17
Shapes ..... 20

**CHAPTER 3: PREPARATION**
Hand Strength ..... 23
Equipment ..... 25
Sensitivity ..... 28

**CHAPTER 4: BASIC LOCKS**
Hand / Wrist ..... 34
Legs ..... 39
Arms ..... 41
Chokes ..... 44

**CHAPTER 5: TAKE DOWNS**
Spine ..... 49
Balance ..... 51
Head ..... 53
Body ..... 59
Legs ..... 61
Counters ..... 70

**CHAPTER 6: THROWS**
Lifts ..... 74
Levers ..... 75
Body Weight ..... 76
Scissors ..... 77
Training Throws ..... 78

**CHAPTER 7: PINS & CARRIES**
Solo Work ..... 83
Partner Work ..... 94

**CHAPTER 8: EQUIPMENT**
Fixed ..... 101
Flexible ..... 109

**CHAPTER 9: UN/FRIENDLY WORK**
Assistance ..... 117
Joint Breaks ..... 121
Pressure Points ..... 123

**CHAPTER 10: ESCAPES**
The Four Pillars ..... 131
One Joint Up ..... 134
Pain Compliance ..... 137
Applied Holds ..... 128

**CHAPTER 11: PROGRESSION**
Advanced Techniques ..... 152
Refinement ..... 154
Wave ..... 158
Movement ..... 161
Integration ..... 163
Density ..... 167
Internal Work ..... 170
Non Contact Work ..... 180
Precision ..... 187

**CHAPTER 12: DRILLS**
Variables ..... 190
Drill Types ..... 193

**CHAPTER 13: CONCLUSIONS**

# CHAPTER ONE
# INTRODUCTION

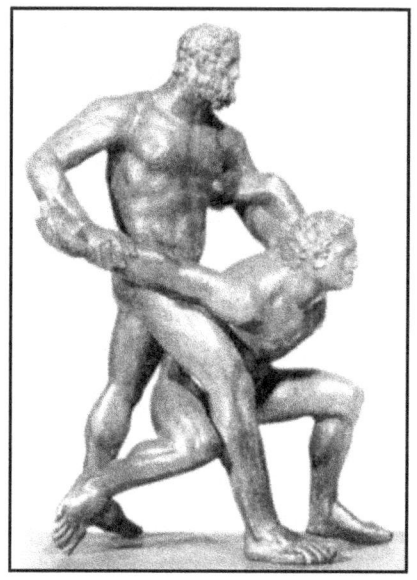

How can you subdue an attacker without injuring them? It's a question asked over generations and, perhaps, one reason that civilian martial arts developed in the first place. We know that *martial* means *war,* which conjures up images of warriors on the battlefield engaged in life or death combat with weapons. There would appear to be little use for restraint work there. Yet even in a military context, it may be necessary to subdue rather than kill. Perhaps a prisoner needs to be taken? Perhaps a member of your own unit needs to be restrained?

Outside of the military, there are numerous situations that call for the application of *soft force*. An LEO making an arrest, door staff keeping people safe in a nightclub, a drunken friend at a social occasion, and so on. However the question remains - how to subdue without injury? The answer is often *not very easily*!

Restraining an aggressive, active person is no mean feat and calls for a high level of skill and calmness. But why not just pop the attacker one on the jaw? Or knock them out with a chop to the neck? Those may be options in the movies but there is another reason for being proficient at soft-force too, and that is safety. Numerous people fall victim to the so called "one punch kill, " where a single blow knocks a person over, causing death from the impact of their head hitting the floor.

The problem is exacerbated by the common perception of martial artists - that we are all combat experts, able to subdue the craziest, knife-wielding attacker simply by tapping a pressure point on the arm. There have been numerous cases in the UK where a martial artist acted correctly (in my view) yet was penalised in court for being "too rough" with the attacker. In fact, in that situation I would be wary about even mentioned that I trained in martial arts, it is likely to count against you.

Given all these factors, it is very important that anyone interested in civilian self defence have some knowledge of locks, holds and take downs.

If we think about it, grappling is one of the oldest, if not the oldest, form of martial art; prevalent in every culture, universal in application from sporting to combative. A good thing about grappling work is that unlike striking and weapons work, it can be trained at reasonably high intensity without too much risk of injury. Training it also helps with attribute development, including good understanding of body mechanics, sensitivity, correct use of strength, developing endurance and so on.

Plus, it can be fun, too! Animals learn by wrestling and so do humans! Kids naturally grapple as part of their development. It may have also been the case, or still is in some societies, that wrestling is a social activity too, a way of inter-acting with our peers and building bonds. There is also a cross-over between grappling and massage and health practices

**THE SYSTEMA APPROACH**

We can broadly divide grapple training into two approaches - technique and principles. Systema, as developed and taught by Mikhail Ryabko and Vladimir Vasiliev, takes the latter, with the occasional technique peppered in here and there. My own experience is that this approach develops students much quicker and gives more breadth to their skills. Principles are universal, meaning that skills we develop are applicable to all types of work. This takes away the need to study a separate striking art, grappling art, weapons art plus some form of health work. In Systema we have everything contained in one package.

In that sense, then, the Systema approach to grappling is no different to the Systema approach to striking or using a pistol. The Four Pillars of breathing, movement, form and relaxation give shape to our methods and the overall mental approach should be one of adaptability, willingness to experiment and playfulness.

I mentioned play earlier. Some people in martial arts are sometimes put off by the word "playful," yet this describes some aspects of our training perfectly. The method where a single technique is worked over and over, is said to take thousands of repetitions to become "natural." Yet we already have a perfectly good set of natural reactions and attributes. The playful approach helps put us back in touch with these attributes and, consequently, it takes far less time to develop skills. In that sense, Systema is often said to be about *taking away* rather than *adding*. In other words, removing the learnt or developed inhibitors to those natural skills

Whichever approach we use in training, the safety of all involved is a primary concern. One very noticeable difference between Systema and other grappling methods is that we do not tap. In other arts, when a lock is applied to biting point, the recipient taps in order to say "that's enough" and the lock is released. This is not something we encourage in Systema, for two main reasons.

Firstly, we feel that any discomfort felt should be countered with acceptance and breathing rather than by "surrender." Secondly, we feel that the person applying the lock should exercise a degree of sensitivity in their work. This turns things around a little from the "conventional" approach. What I mean by that, is that in some schools I have trained at, the goal was to snap a lock on quick and hard, bang the partner to the mat, then stroll away, satisfied with a job well done. I have friends who spent years training this way, sad to say that they carry long-term injuries from such repeated stresses.

In the Systema approach, applying a lock on my partner is an opportunity for him or her to experience some pain and work through it - to learn how to counter it through use of the the Four Pillars. Once they learn how to deal with a certain amount of discomfort, it can be increased next time -

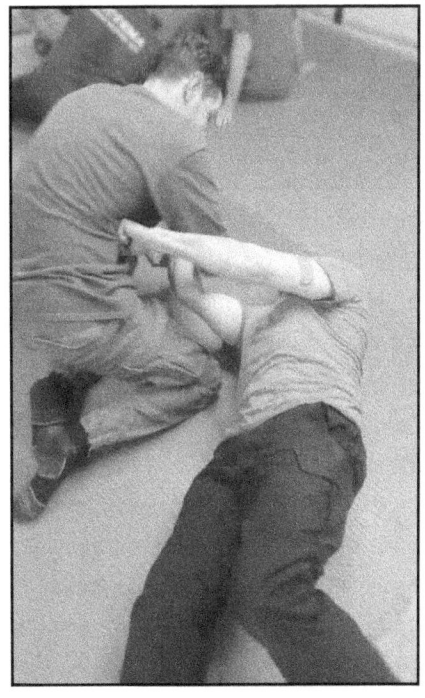

with an obvious upper limit on causing actual damage. This is no different to our approach for taking strikes - it isn't a punishment or chance to show off our hits, it's a graduated method for learning to deal with fear and tension.

So when applying locks, be mindful of the experience of your partner and sensitive to their tension levels. A good clue is to listen to their breathing, that should be a good indicator of their internal state. The same principle applies when we move on to throws and takedowns - work should be graduated according to your partner's ability to fall and manage impact. Falling skills will not be covered here, but will be detailed in a future volume. However, if you are a Systema student I will assume you have some degree of falling skill.

Another difference is the lack of mats, which most grappling styles use. From a Systema perspective, there is nothing wrong with mats as such, particularly for beginners, or if you are trying out some new or heavier work. Having said that, you should aim to move away from mats and onto a normal surface as quickly as possible. We should always be mindful of context in our training. Confrontations take place in all sorts of environments and we should be mentally and physically prepared for that. It's nice to think we can control all these different aspects of a situation, unfortunately we often barely even have control of ourselves!

We should also be aware of training being too cooperative and "nice" all the time, as well. It is important to testing our skills, particularly for any professionals who may have to rely on them in their work. There are numerous methods of doing so within the Systema context. To that end I have included a few testing drills to give you some ideas. Of course, there are also plenty of open competitions available should you wish to test yourself out in a sporting context. From the other angle, Systema has much to offer anyone interested in combat sports.

**HOW TO USE THIS BOOK**

I'm assuming that you have some experience of Systema, or similar arts. To that end, I will not be covering aspects of breathing and posture in detail here - there are more detailed resources available such

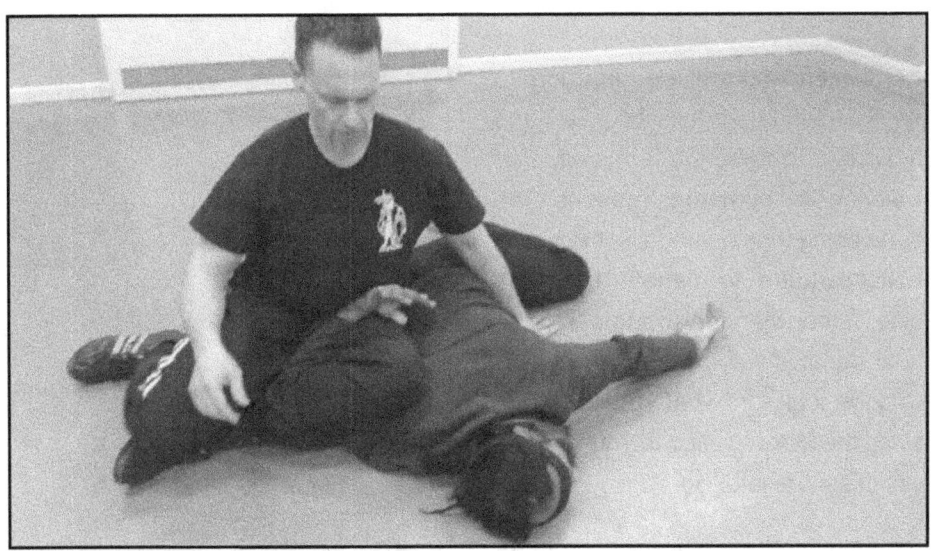

as *Let Every Breath* by Vladimir Vasiliev, for example. Please bear in mind, then, that correct breathing underpins all of the methods presented here - I can't emphasise that enough. I will be sprinkling in occasional reminders of all the Four Pillars, as we go along.

This book is not an encyclopedia of locking techniques. In any case, no single book could cover every single possible technique, variation and situation. It is rather a guide to setting up training drills that will develop your skills. One of the main roles of a Systema Instructor (in my view) is to create the best conditions by which students can learn and grow. That generally takes the form of setting up a drill, where the people work within set parameters designed to help develop specific attributes. Some of these drills look "combative," some don't (as we know by reading You-tube comments!) What they look like is of no importance, the important thing is their function.

Drills are endlessly flexible and can be tweaked in all sorts of ways. I describe this in more depth in my book *The Ten Points of Sparring* but will give you some ideas in a later chapter. All the drills presented here can, and should be, developed by you according to your own abilities and needs. If you are new to this type of training, pick one or two of the basic drills to start with and work from there.

If you are an Instructor or run a training group, I hope you find some new ideas and challenges here for your group. As usual, I will include some background science here but, in order to keep the book as practical as possible, will keep the science basic. I always encourage you to carry out your own further research, though, especially where it enhances understanding.

For convenience, I will be referring to people illustrating that drills as A,B,C and so on. I prefer to avoid the terms *attacker* and *defender* for numerous reasons. The main one being that in our drills, the aim is for both partners to benefit from the exercise, rather than for one to purely be the "test dummy" for the other. To that end, always look for what you can learn by having the locks applied to you - we will discuss this more later on.

This book also details some supplementary exercises and attribute development methods that should help with your training. As far as locks and holds go, here and there, I will detail specific techniques, in order to highlight a technical point or to act as a springboard into more free-style work. Again, I would emphasise that you pay particular attention to the safety and care of both yourself and your partners in training. Apply all the methods slowly to being with, especially if you are trying them for the first time. When working directly against joints, be wary of changing directions at speed and/or under tension - this is where damage can occur. Always work with consideration to your partner's training level. Likewise, never be afraid to say "that's enough" when a lock is applied.

A few more things I would like to mention before we get started. The first is the photographs used in the book. Thanks to everyone who helped on this, both those

who kindly came and "modelled" and to my wife for patiently taking so many of the pics. Generally, I prefer to use photos or video stills from actual training in my books, as I feel they convey a better sense of movement. However, in this book I found it necessary to take a number of very specific pictures in order to illustrate certain techniques or moves. These pics always look a little "staged" to me but hopefully they get the information across. I'm sure there are those who will be able to pick some of them apart on technical grounds but what is important to me is that they convey the essence and underlying principle of the move in question, not give a text-book perfect representation of a classic technique.

The second relates to the fact that, while we operate as complete beings, in training we often parse information down into chunks. Otherwise we would all struggle, especially early on, in trying to match breathing,

psyche, structure, tension levels, technical ability, environmental factors and everything else that goes into the most basic of confrontations. To that end, the work here is divided into sections, particularly when it come to the deeper aspects of training. That may mean I repeat myself here and there but I make no apology for that - some things bear repeating!

The third point relates to the above. All of the work detailed here can be applied on many levels, in particular psychological. I do not talk about this much in the book but ask that you bear it in mind as you work through it. We all understand having an arm locked. But how well do we understand how our own mindset can often lock us, too?

Then we can broaden that out to understand control mechanisms, how we are influenced through our emotional "pressure points" and how sometimes quite subtle restrictions shape our lives and activities. This may be from family members, the workplace, or society as a whole, especially in these days of instant mass communication. Of course, we accept some of these things as being part of a healthy society but any principle is just that - how it is used another question.

One last point. Systema is perhaps unique in that people can train in it while injured. Indeed, I would encourage you to do so, depending on medical advice. Drills can be adapted to suit most conditions. In this sense, think of your injury as a lock or a hold. Whatever your issues (and they seem to increase with age!), find ways to work around them, much as you learn to move while someone is grabbing you.

If you have any questions, please get in touch via Facebook or e-mail. And, of course, for more detailed and in-depth training, visit Moscow and/or Toronto HQ or attend any of the numerous seminars that are now world-wide. It remains only for me to thanks my teachers, Mikhail Ryabko and Vladimir Vasiliev (all the good things in my books are from the them, the rest is mine)

# CHAPTER TWO
# MECHANICS

We are going to start by looking at some body structures and mechanics. On the most basic level, holds work on a bio-mechanical level. There are other factors involved too, which we shall discuss later on. However, to begin with, it is useful to know a few basic shapes and simple mechanical principles. The body is an incredible machine. Our muscular and skeletal systems work together to move it. Aspects of that movement can be thought of as *simple machines*. There are six types of simple machine. They are the foundation blocks from which all more complicated machines are composed. These six are the lever, wheel and axle, pulley, inclined plane, wedge and screw.

On a bio-mechanical level, these give us a guide as to how our bodies work and also how they may be manipulated for purposes of restraint. Let's examine each in turn.

## LEVER

A lever is a bar that turns on an unmoving point, or *fulcrum*. Pressure applied to one end of the is called *the input force* or *effort*.

The object lifted at the other end is called *the load* or *the output force*. These are the three parts of every lever.

There are three types of levers: first, second, and third class. The difference between the three depends on the position of the effort, fulcrum and load.

In a first class lever, the fulcrum is located between the effort and load - think of a see-saw.

In a second class lever, the load is between the fulcrum and the effort - such as in a wheelbarrow.

In a third class lever, the effort is between the fulcrum and the load - sweeping a broom, for example.

The obvious levers in the body are the arms. We normally think of a lever as something that helps us to hold or move large loads. However, another function of levers is to increase range of motion. If we take the forearm and lifting a ball as an example, the force provided by the biceps has to be much larger than the weight of the

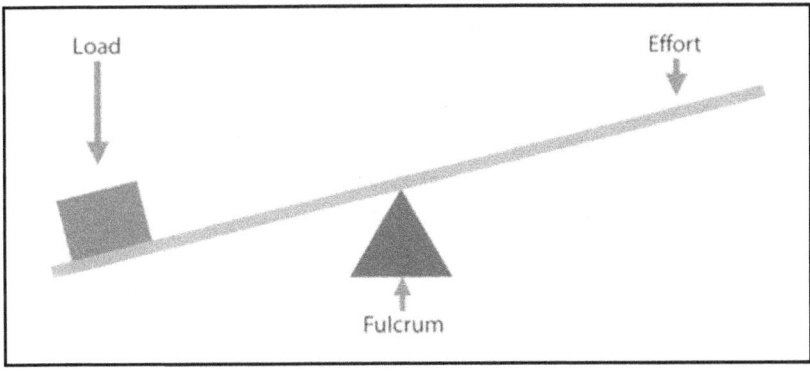

ball, which seems at odds with our previous functions. But if If we look instead at at how far the ball moves compared to how far the biceps contract when lifting, we see that the purpose of the forearm lever is to increase range of motion rather than decrease effort required. In effect, the lever magnifies our movement.

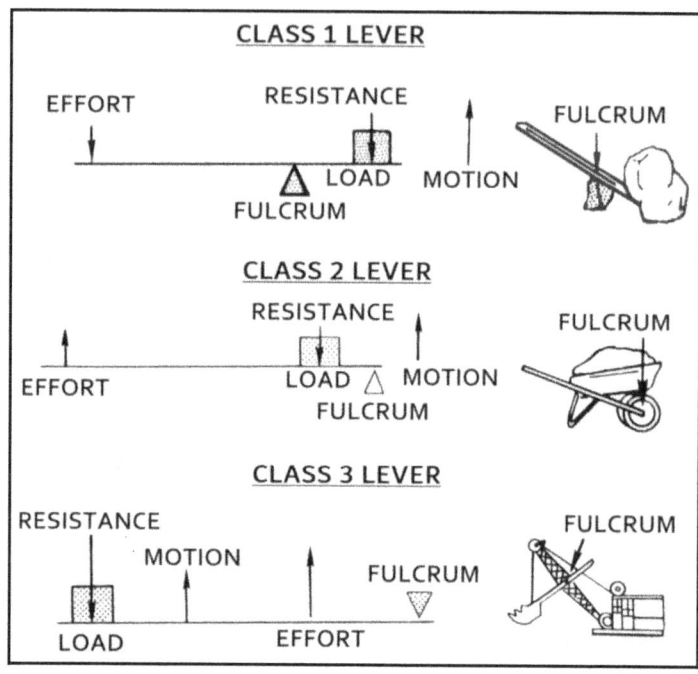

## WHEEL

A wheel can work to either multiply force or speed, but not both at the same time. If you turn the rim of a wheel, the axle at the centre turns with less speed but more force, making the wheel a force multiplier. If you turn the axle (as in a car), the wheel becomes a speed multiplier. The axle turns only a short distance but leverage makes the outer rim turn much further in the same time.

Wheels are used to multiply force in other ways, too. When you turn the outer rim of a stopcock, the inner axle turns with much greater force, making the pipe is easier to close. A lorry has a bigger steering wheel than a car, because it takes more force to turn its wheels. The bigger wheel gives the driver more leverage.

Wheelbarrows combine wheels and levers to brilliant effect, making it easy to transport loads. Its long frame acts like a lever, making the load easier to lift. And it is easier to push the load because the only friction is between the wheel and the axle.

We don't have wheels in the body as such, the closest we can think of are ball and socket joints. However we can use the concept of the wheel in our movement.

## PULLEY

A pulley is a wheel that carries a flexible rope, cord, cable, or similar on its rim. Pulleys are used singly or in combination to transmit energy and motion.

Pulley systems within the body make many difficult tasks simpler. The psoas muscle acts like a pulley and so do the quadriceps. Our legs are designed to track directly over the ankles when we walk and run. This is one of the main distinctions of being upright and walking on two legs.

## WEDGE

A wedge is an object that tapers to a thin edge. Pushing the wedge in one direction creates a force in a sideways direction. It is usually made of metal or wood and is used for splitting, lifting, or tightening, as in securing a hammer head onto its handle. One type of wedge in the body are the teeth.

## INCLINED PLANE

An inclined plane consists of a sloping surface, often used for raising heavy bodies. The plane offers a mechanical advantage in that the force required to move an object up the incline is less than the weight that is being raised - discounting friction. The steeper the slope, or incline, the more nearly the required force approaches the actual weight.

Our feet have an inclined plane on the surface and underneath them. Our feet can hold up tons of weight, and the inclined plane helps to keep us balanced and sturdy. In fact, having "flat feet" is actually a medical problem.

## SCREW

A screw is a circular cylindrical object or movement, used either as a fastener or as a force and motion modifier. It converts rotational motion to linear motion, and a torque (rotational force) to a linear force. In terms of the body, we can think of how the muscles wrap around the bones and how we can generate force through spiraling movements.

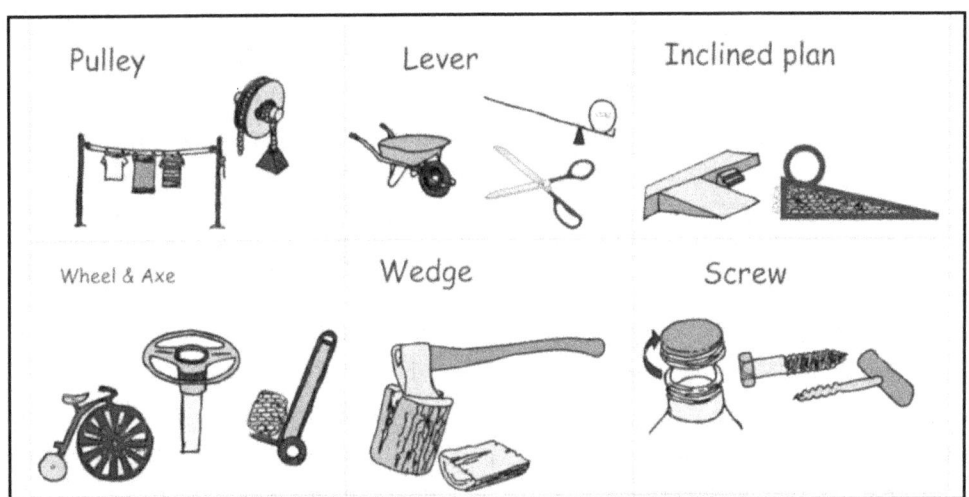

## SHAPES AND MOVEMENT

Understanding certain shapes or structures will improve our locks and holds and enhance the work of our simple machines. The two principles combined allow us to work with much less overt strength or tension and so get a greater effect for less effort.

## TRIANGLE

Many joint locks, particularly smaller ones, work from the application of leverage in a triangle shape. Let's take the classic police transport wrist-lock as an example. Imagine a right-angled triangle superimposed over the arm. We are trying to take the point of the shortest side along the hypotenuse. Keeping two of the corners corners fixed in place increases the effectiveness - in this case, one with the hand, the other with the body. This may be a small triangle, in the case of a finger lock, or it may cover the whole limb.

## CIRCLE

Another application of shapes is to think of them as movement. This time, let's use a basic arm bar. Again, you see that we are applying leverage to the elbow joint. We can press straight down and will probably get a result - though it may take a fair amount of force. If we add in circular movement, we will find that far less force is required. The human body does not respond well to circular force. If you want to test this out, try this experiment.

A holds their fist out in front and tenses the arm. B presses on the fist in one direction - up, down or two the side. Build the pressure up rather than applying it quickly. If A is reasonably strong, they should be able to fix the fist in place using tension, it does not move. B can ease off and try a different direction. In itself, this is the basis of one of our selective tension exercises.

Reset and try again. This time, rather than press in a straight line, B adds a curve to the pressure - to the side and up, for example. This time B will find it virtually impossible to maintain the position of the fist. In fact, B should be able to move the fist with only light finger pressure.

Having tried that, go back to the basic arm bar. This time, as you press down on or just above the elbow, add in a forward rotation (slowly). You should find the lock becomes much more difficult to resist.

## WAVE

The wave is a staple of Systema movement. You can think of it as a ripple or whip effect through the body. To feel it, wave your right hand and allow the movement to travel up the arm, across the shoulders, down the left arm and out of the left hand. When applied to locks, the wave principle will increase effectiveness while lessening the need for tension or force.

Let's use the example of another classic wrist lock, known as *kote gaeshi* in the Japanese arts. Place the thumbs on the back of your partners wrist and bend, bearing in mind our training shape from before. This, in itself, may suffice. If there is strong resistance, though, you can try using the circle method from above.

Another option is to "wave". Set up that ripple across the shoulders as described above. This will naturally add in a circle to your movement, but also add extra directions, too. In effect, you can wave the hand back and forth, creating a whiplash effect. Be sure to practice this slowly at first. if carried out at speed the effect on the joints can be devastating.

## SPIRAL

Spirals can be inherent in waves. Try the hand - shoulder-hand wave from above but this time add in a rotation of the arms. The movement should feel less "wavy" and a little more focused. Let's use our basic arm-bar again to illustrate. One hand holds the wrist, the other applies force as before. Of course, we can add the circle or wave in. To spiral, we first twist with the grabbing hand - this should be the thumb travelling up if we are using a conventional grip. Not just up, but also pushing inward, up along the grabbed arm.

At the same time, the pressing arm also spirals, again the thumb rotating up. Think of it as cutting into the locked arm with your ulna. The combination of the two spirals can create a lot of pressure on the arm with little apparent effect, so again, proceed with care.

In reality we may use any or several of the above simultaneously. Leverage is the most common application but, as we have seen, we can add other shapes into even a basic lever to increase its effectiveness. We will show how other aspects of shape and movement can work as we progress. For now, we will move onto some preparation work for training locks and holds.

# CHAPTER THREE
# PREPARATION

Any type of work needs a combination of physical preparedness, attribute development and technical skill in order to be effective. In holds and lock terms, all the usual Systema methods apply - strengthening the body through our core exercises, training mobility, good use of structure, efficient breathing and so on. However, there are a few things that are more specific to grappling skills, so lets start with some key preparation exercises

While not exclusively, the vast majority of locks and holds involve us grabbing something - so it makes sense that a strong grip will improve our work. There are numerous methods for training grip but the first thing to consider is hand / finger mobility. In Systema, mobility is as important a component as strength, we are always aware of maintaining the correct balance between the two. Likewise, we must also retain an element of sensitivity in our grip, in order to be able adapt to changing situations.

## HAND STRETCHES

Rub the hands together. Shake them a few times. Lock the fingers together and rotate the wrists. Open and close the fists a few times.

Lay your hand out flat on a table or solid surface. Use your other hand to slowly lift up a finger, keeping the rest of your fingers flat. Lift and stretch the finger as high as it will go without straining. Breathe. Hold for a few seconds and slowly release it back down. Repeat on all fingers and thumb.

While standing, place your palms together in a praying position. Have your elbows touch each other. Your hands should be in front of your face. Your arms should be touching each other from the tips of your fingers to your elbows. With your palms pressed together, slowly spread your elbows apart. Do this while lowering your hands to waist height. Stop when your hands are in front of your belly button or you feel the stretch. Hold for 10 to 30 seconds.

Extend one arm in front of you at shoulder height. Keep your palm down, facing the floor. Release your wrist so that your fingers

point downward. With your free hand, gently grasp your fingers and pull them back toward your body. Hold for 10 to 30 seconds.

Extend your arm with your palm facing up toward the ceiling. With your free hand, gently press your fingers down toward the floor. Gently pull your fingers back toward your body. Hold for 10 to 30 seconds.

Get into push up position, or at first you can kneel on the floor and lean forward, making a square with your hands and knees. Places palms flat on the floor, fingers pointing forward. Now begin to point the fingers in different directions, so the hands can be forward, sideways or tow ards your feet. Turn one or both palms up so you that your wrists are on the floor. Lean weight into the wrists or try full push ups- gauge it according to your wrist strength and flexibility. Next, place the back of the hands to the floor and lean weight or do push ups again.

## HAND STRENGTH

Begin by pinching the tips of your fingers and thumbs. Put an elastic band around your fingers. Move your fingers away from your thumb so that the band becomes tight. Extend your fingers and thumb away and close to each other 10 times.

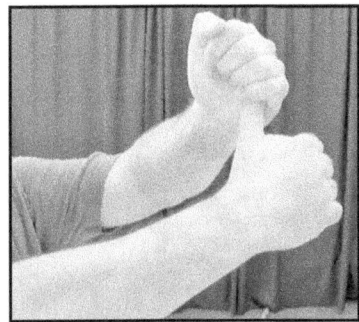

While seated, place your palms face up under a desk or table. Press upwards against the bottom of the desk. Hold for 5 to 10 seconds.

Make a fist and point your thumb up, as if you're giving a thumbs-up sign. Create resistance with your thumb and hand muscles to keep your thumb from moving. Gently pull back on your thumb with your free hand. Hold and repeat. You can work this method with all the fingers

Stand a short distance away from a wall. Raise your heels and lean your palms onto the wall for support. Now move from palms to fingers - either singly or both hands. With the weight resting on your fingers, move around the wall (like Spiderman). Repeat facing away from the wall.

**EQUIPMENT**

Our next set of exercises use equipment. This doesn't have to be anything too specialised, you can improvise with household items in most cases. Almost anything with a bit of weight can be used, as long as you bear safety in mind.

Squeeze a tennis ball or stress ball firmly for 5 to 10 seconds.

Place the hands over a jar or jug, grip with the fingers, lift and carry. Over time, increase the load by gradually filling the item with water, sand, stones, etc.

Rather than carry, you can work drop and catch. Depending on the object, I'd advise working on a soft surface or placing a cushion below it and keeping your feet well out of the way!

You can use a brick, a hammer, and so on. For something more demanding, try a heavy ball - a shot put, for example Simply drop and catch the ball. Work each hand equally, gradually build up reps. As a progression, you can make the ball harder to grip. Try getting it chromed and, after that, put a thin layer of cooking oil on it!

Any good movement with the stick, sword or sledge hammer will help develop the hands. For specific work, hold the stick at one end. Keep it parallel to the floor. Now drop and catch, moving the hand along a little each time. So you work from one end of the stick to the other.

If you have a pair of short sticks, use them like chopsticks to pick up a heavy object. Progress by varying the weight, hand position and moving around while holding the object.

Hold the stick vertically between a finger of each hand. Start at one end and "walk" the fingers to the other end. As a progression, try this with a hammer or sledgehammer.

A towel is a useful bit of kit for grip training. If you have a long towel you can try pull ups. Make sure you grip each side of the towel evenly. There's variations of this exercise, depending on what kind of pull up bar or equipment you have. Drape the towel over it in as many different ways as you can and try pulls up from each position.

With a shorter towel, you can try wringing exercises. Fill a bucket or basin with water, and submerge the

towel in it for a couple of minutes. Next, take the towel out, keeping it over the water. Start to squeeze and twist the towel as tightly as you can. Be sure that all the water you wring out of the towel goes back into the bucket. The object is to squeeze all of the water out of the towel so that the water level ends up the same as when you started.

Rope is another great item. You can use it for pull ups as with the towel. You can also use ropes for climbing, of course. If you really want to work fingers, then unpick a rope, or try unpicking knots in string. If that gets too easy, soak them in water beforehand!

Tearing, ripping and bending can be practiced with any suitable object. Put several sheets of paper together and tear them in half. Put all the halves together and rip again. I don't suppose they make telephone directories any more, but people used to rip those in half! You can try bending nails, crushing apples or perhaps beer cans (unfortunately you have to empty them first). Just be aware of safety and dispose of your waste responsibly.

You can buy hand grippers, two handles joined by a spring of varying strength. Start with one of the lower ones ( usually around 60-80lbs of pressure). Use is easy - simply squeeze the handles together - and they are highly portable.

Perhaps the best type of equipment to work with is a partner! As well strength we also get benefits of sensitivity with these exercises.

Stand opposite and link little fingers. Each partner applies equal pull to the other, building up gradually. Work through each finger in turn. Link all the fingers together and apply gentle pressure, keeping the hands relaxed. Work into different angles and positions. Repeat but this time apply more tension / resistance. Work slowly

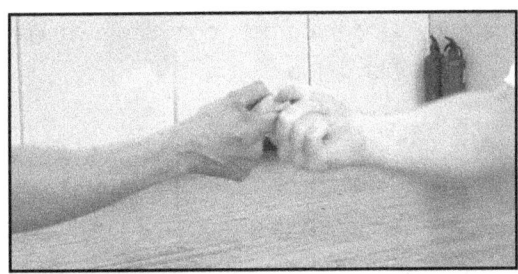

and make sure the tension remains in the forearms, the rest of the body should be mobile and relaxed. Again, move around into different positions and change levels.

You can do the same type of drill with a hand clasp. From the start position one person applies pressure and the other gives resistance, a kind of mobile arm wrestling. Start with a single hand, then work both. As before, add in your level changes and different start positions.

Of course, you can combine equipment and a partner. Each holds one end of a stick, rope or towel and twists in opposite directions. Add in an extra partner to work both hands at the same time.

## SENSITIVITY

Our hands are incredibly sensitive. If you look at a picture of an adult homunculus (the representation of how much of the brain controls different areas of the body), you will see that the hands are enormous. This show what a big part of the brain is devoted to the hands. If you think about it, we use our hands almost constantly in daily life, including many tasks that involve fine motor skills

Chances are that with eyes closed, you could tell what an object placed in your hand is - say, a coin, an apple. This ability is known as *stereognosis*. That can be our start point - simply identify different items while blindfold. Feel every aspect of the

item - the texture, the shape, the weight. What is its consistency, its temperature? When you start to examine it, the sense of touch involves more factors than you may think. Carry this over into everyday life. Take time not just to touch, but to feel.

Using a ball is a great way to develop sensitivity. It can be anything from Chinese health balls up to a football or beach ball. Simply roll the ball around and maintain an even contact with it. You can roll the ball against a wall, or around the body.

Another good exercise for "following movement" is to use a stick. Balance it upright in the hand then try and keep it steady. Once you get good, begin walking around with it, too.

You can try exercises with a pen or coin - roll them between the fingers. Any kind of activity requiring fine motor skills will help too, such as drawing, painting, making

models, crafts, manipulating playing cards and so on.

As well as these exercises, look for other activities that will improve hand strength and coordination. Some of the strongest grips I've felt have been from climbers - which calls not only for strength but also feeling! Indoor climbing walls are available at most sports centres now. Good, old-fashioned manual labour is another strength developer. Probably the overall strongest grip I ever felt was from an older chap who had spent years working as a navvy. So every day he was digging, moving things around building sites and so on. He had a grip like steel!

## SUPPLENESS

Free movement serves two purposes. It allows us to apply our holds freely and from unusual positions. It also helps condition us for receiving locks. This is important not only for counter work but also for general training. Much like strikes or throws, the better we can deal with them, the more intensely our partners can work. You have to be much more careful when you work with a partner who is very tense and not used to dealing with impact or grabs. That is fine to start but once you move into the testing or free-play and sparring stages it is important for each student to be able to protect themselves to some extent.

Let's start with solo twisting movements. Simply grab one hand with the other and begin twisting. Work slowly, breath, relax into the twist. Feel the limit of what you can take and see if you can (safely) extend it. Do the same with your feet. Look at how you can use the body to fix a hand or leg in place to help twist the shoulder, for example.

Next, lay on the floor and begin twisting and stretching out. Extend a hand and foot as far as you can, twisting as you do so. This, in itself, should give you a very nice stretch. Work in as many different directions and positions as you can.

Other solo suppleness work includes any of the usual joint rotations, figure eight, wave work and stretching that are part of regular Systema training.

## LEVEL CHANGE

Some locks or throws are applied by using our body weight. In these cases we usually fall quickly to the floor, taking our partner with us. Also, when escaping locks we may sometimes need to duck, drop or even roll. It makes sense, then, to be used to level change. The usual Systema falls and rolls work is good preparation for this and there are some other things you might like to try too. Walk around your training space and periodically change height. Drop into a duck walk, got to the floor and roll and so on. Once you are able to transition smoothly, run the same exercise again, but this time holding a stick or similar object. This represents the fact that you may be holding onto someone when you change level. In other words, learn to drop without using your hands.

**WARM UPS**

There are a number of partner drills we can use as part of a warm up for any lock/throw session. As is usually the case in Systema, these drills are multi-functional, developing more than the attributes directly related to the specific topic. These drills also act as a good starting point for working into application work.

Let's first go back to our earlier twisting exercises. However much we can twist alone, a partner can always get a little more movement out of those muscles! So now, take a partner's hand and begin slowly twisting. At first, work in an upright, comfortable position (or on the floor for the legs). Take the hand or foot to the point where you feel tension - and listen for the burst breathing. Hold that position and allow your partner to relax into it. Much like our stretching work, relaxing the muscle will bring a little more movement. Never force movement, also be sure never to change direction quickly, always be sensitive to your partner.

There is a physical aspect to this work but also a strong psychological one. Fear from the twisted limb can bring tension into the psyche. This in turn tenses the muscles more, creating a vicious circle. So as well as a muscle relaxant, use this drill to practice control of your mind. Use whichever breathing method suits best -usually burst breathing for more intense pain. This will dampen down the signals from the nervous system and help keep us clam and in control. If you would like to take this aspect further, you can work with four people each twisting a limb - as detailed in our *Systema Awareness* book.

Once you have the static version down, begin adding in some movement. Let's take the hand as an example. A twists B's fingers

and wrist. B must allow the twist to bite and control any fear or tension that results. B must now see how much movement they have in the rest of the body. Can you rotate your shoulders? Move your hips and step? The aim is to keep any tension from the twist from travelling up the arm. From the wrist, move up to the shoulder and work the same procedure. B then lays down and the same work is applied to the legs.

A good drill for general movement is to use a stick. A grabs one end and must hold on to the stick as B moves them around. To start, B makes simple movements, working slow. As A relaxes and loosens up the movements can become more challenging. Change level, add in some twists and spirals, change direction more frequently. The movements don't have to be super-fast and keep them smooth - the aim is to challenge A's movement, not rip the stick from their grasp.

Our final warm up drill is the grab and escape, a standard of most of our classes. At the simplest level, A applies a grab towards B, who must evade it. Once again, slow and smooth is the way to start. The grab can be to any part of the body. B must evade as fluidly as possible, keeping good form or getting back into it quickly if they have to break. Check how good use of footwork makes it easier for you to keep form. You can add in deflection movements with the hands, if you like. For the next level, have B escape from the grab then come back in with one of their own. In other words, partner's worth back and forth in an exchange of grabs.

# CHAPTER FOUR
# BASIC LOCKS

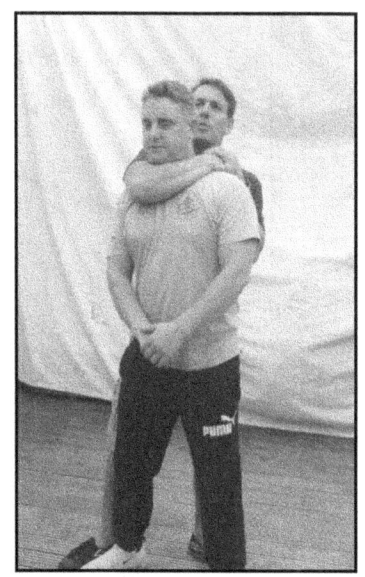

Let's next start looking at how to apply simple locks and holds. We will broadly divide our work into three areas, small and large joint locks and holds (chokes and restraints.) Remember again to carry out all work slowly and with care.

We also need to consider the purpose of the lock. At workshops, I sometimes ask people why they strike. Most struggle to give an answer - in a fight, you punch someone, right? My point is, what are you trying to achieve with this punch? Knock-out? Stun? Break? Relax? Agitate? Strikes have more uses than people may think. Likewise with locks and holds. We must know what we are trying to achieve when applying our work.

knee may allow us to escape without risk of pursuit, for example.

There are normally three goals when working locks. Restrain, transport, damage.

Restraint is where we need to fix someone in place. We need to prevent them moving around, for their own or other's protection. It could be we need to pin them in order to apply cuffs, for example, or perhaps prevent them from moving somewhere else.

Transport is where we need to get a person from A to B. To escort them out of a club, say.

Damage is where the aim is to apply sufficient force to actual injure the person. So breaking a bone, popping a joint. This is obviously for more serious situations where our life is under threat. Breaking a

Each of these is closely linked. Usually, in order to transport a person you have to restrain them, in some way. Quite often we even use the same movement or technique. We should also always bear in mind that any lock is also a break - it's just a question of degree. Bend a finger far enough and it snaps. That may or may not be required according to the situation - there's no one size fits all rule.

## SMALL JOINT LOCKS

In some ways, SJL are the simplest. Everyone knows how to bend back a finger, right? The problem is that a simple finger lock may not be enough to subdue an attacker. However, they are useful for low level situations and also serve as a good exercise in placement and precision. At a more advanced stage, SJL can be extremely effective against the most determined of attackers and can be used for restraint or throws.

**FINGERS AND WRIST**

We start with a simple drill. A takes B's hand and begins working each finger individually. See how much movement there is in each finger before tension sets in. Move the finger up, down sideways. Now repeat, but this time work the joints in the fingers. Curl the finger in on itself and see what effect that has. Obviously we are doing all of this with care. At this stage B should be static. The third stage is to work with two or more fingers. Squeeze them together, bend and twist as before.

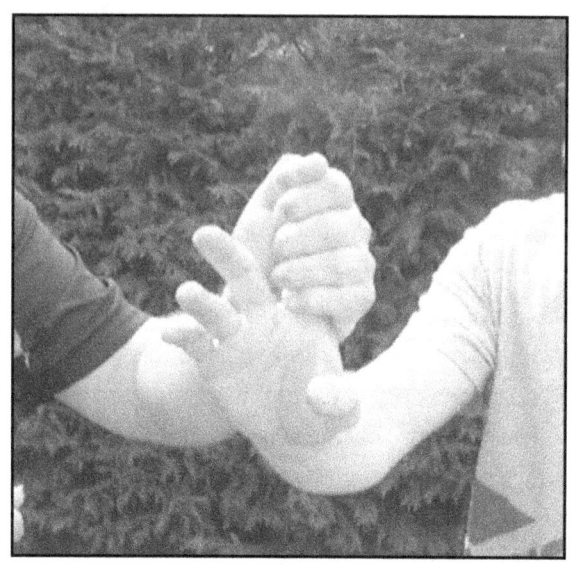

This starts to teach us the movement tolerance of the fingers. Now, let's add in some movement. B comes to A with a simple grab. Pre-contact, A shifts the body, takes B's fingers and applies a basic lock. It is good for A to start working in their own movement even at this stage - movement is our primary defence in Systema. Match the movement to the attack. In case of a lapel grab, just shift slight back and rotate a little to the side. You want the person to keep grabbing.

This concept highlights another important Systema principle - acceptance. In this case, we are accepting that the grab is coming in. One reaction might be to try and knock the grabbing hand away, but this is usually a reaction born out of fear. Instead, we respond by taking the hand that our attacker has so kindly given us. We should look upon the attack as an opportunity. Our body movement should also be a smooth response, not a jerky fear-based reaction.

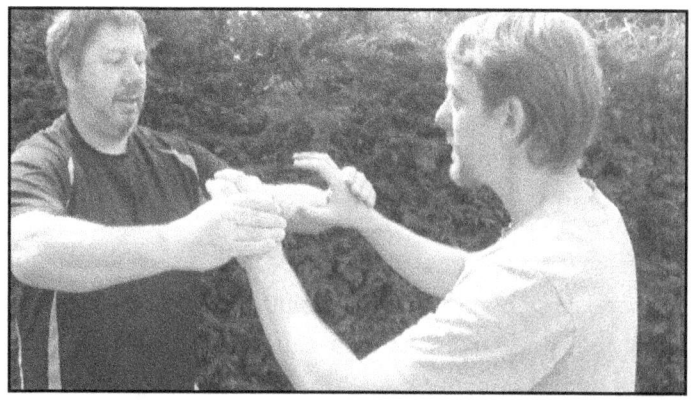

So that's the basic drill, let's look at few refinements.

## GRABBING FINGERS

It's tempting to grab fingers in the "wrestling" way - in other words, we interlock our fingers with those of the attacker. This tends to put us in a 50-50 situation, our attacker has as much positional advantage as we do. Instead, bring your grab in from the sides. Let's use a double hand grab to illustrate.

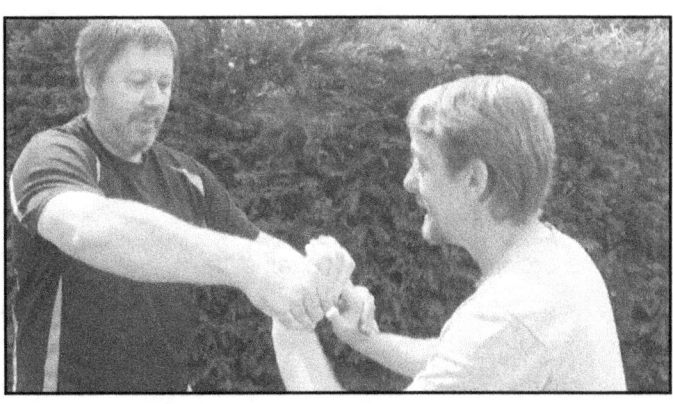

A comes in to grab B's shirt-front. B angles their body slightly and curves their own hands in from the sides - keep them at the same level or slightly under A's hands. The grab should be with the thumbs in the inside and the fingers on top. From here, rotate your thumbs up to apply downward force into the fingers. Done correctly, you will bring A to their knees. Be sure not to use tense force when you do this, simply bend forward a little - remember, the power is in the movement, not the muscles.

You can amplify the effect of this move by also turning your waist. Lift one of the attacker's arms higher than the other as you do so and the lock becomes a throw.

Another version of to use two hands against one grabbing hand. In this case, each hand grabs with the same circular method, this time each grabbing two or three fingers. From there, bend as before or, for a more damaging response, pull the fingers apart.

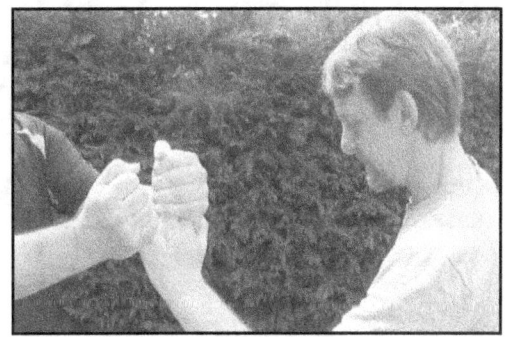

Another refinement is not even to grab the fingers but to push on them. This takes good timing but is surprisingly effective. This item, as the grab comes in you place your palms on the fingertips and push forward

and down. Done correctly, it will lock the fingers, then that tension will go up into the wrist and arms. Again, direct the attacker downward.

But what if the grab has actually come on? Well, one option is still to work against the fingers. One way to do this is to "peel" a finger off of the grip and bend it. By the way, should you wish to break a finger, it is best to bend it sideways rather than back, there is less tolerance that way.

Another method is to use a standard martial arts technique, usually known as Centre Lock. A has grabbed B by the shirt. B covers A's hand with their own. The first work is against the thumb. Bearing in mind our triangle principle. B squeezes thumb inwards to create pain. This may, or may not, be enough to loosen the grip (we will talk more about pain compliance later).

Next, B squeezes their hand tightly, compressing A's fist. B next rotates the body (if the grab is on the left chest, we rotate right.) As they do so, B rotates there own thumb upwards, turning A's hand a little - but keeping it in contact with the body. Now we use the body as a point of support. B bends forward slightly and raises their thumb. This should lock A's wrist and send that tension up into the arm. Once again, the force is directed downwards.

As I said, this is a "bread and butter" technique across most martial arts styles but it is worth practicing until you can do it smoothly. It highlights some important principles and will lead us on to some other ideas and methods. Once again, do not apply tension, let your movement do the work. Also work slow to start, this move can put a lot of force into the wrist.

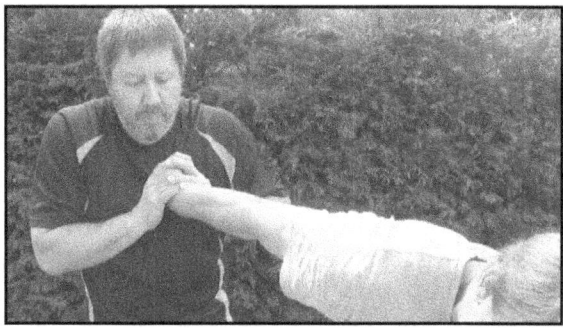

As we have worked into the wrist with that technique, let's look at some more wrist locks. Again, we start with a standard, the police carry or goose neck as it it sometimes known. There's a lot of ways to get in to this particular lock, for now we will focus on the basic position.

A stands to the right side of B and pushes B's elbow up into the chest - not too high, just below the pec is good. B' s other hand covers A's wrist. Now simply apply pressure in and down with the covering hand. The other hand can also come up to the wrist for increased pressure. Be sure to get the angle of the pressure right. Think back to our triangle principle, short side to long side. Be sure that the elbow is tucked firmly into the body, it should not be sliding about. Again, a basic technique but be sure you can do this smoothly, on both sides, before moving on.

Now we have a few ideas for finger and wrist locks, let's work back into a drill. A comes in with grabs on B - simple and slow to start. B's job is avoid the grabs and apply a finger or wrist lock. You don't have to apply the exact techniques form above. Think, though, what they teach us. Use that knowledge to work. See how you can apply torque, how you can put pressure directly onto a joint, how you can create tension through a small lock that travels up the arm. Be creative but keep things simple for now.

Once you have done that drill, run the same thing again but this time work from a position of having been grabbed. So A now grabs your shirt, holds your wrist and so on. See if you can bring the same principles to bear. We will be covering escapes form holds in more detail later but this is good preparation for that work.

Our last drill in this section is to work backwards and forwards. Think of this as a flow drill. A locks B's fingers. However don't apply the lock fully, allow B to escape out just at the last moment. B must then respond with their own lock. You should do this work slowly, give each other a little time to think. Of course, you can also be moving, changing level and so on.

Once again, at this stage this a sensitivity and flow drill, not a wrestling match. Use it to explore positioning, direction change and as a method of checking your own and your partner's tension levels.

One key to putting on locks is the ability to work smoothly, without stimulating the other person's nervous system, working under the radar, as it were. This circumvents a lot of problems with resistance and also "looks better" from an appropriate force perspective. A lock that is on before anyone knows it, comes across much better than a doorman or LEO struggling with someone, perhaps having to hit them, before getting a hold on.

## THE KNIFE

A knife is a very good tool for learning how to lock the hand. Here's a few simple drills that you will find useful.

A holds the knife and B has to take it from them. This works in three stages. First, A applies very little resistance. This gets B used to positioning. Second, A applies moderate resistance. This forces B to

refine their position and movement. Third, A applies full resistance. Now B really has to work hard to get the knife. They may have to use the body as an anchor point and so on. Please note that all A is doing in this drill is holding the knife - no cutting or other movements.

Run the same drill again. This time, the aim is not so much for B to take the knife, but to lock up A's hand / arm. This allows B to try all the previous methods for locks, plus the extra one of using the knife as leverage. Again, run through the three levels of resistance.

You can run the same drill with a stick or any other suitable object. This is also useful preparation for learning how to use a stick for restraint, more on that later on.

## LEG LOCKS

I'm going to spend a little time on the legs, though not as much as the upper body. The reason is that leg locks are more in the domain of ground fighting. Obviously that is an important area, one not to be neglected, but is something we will cover in more detail in a future book. Having said that, it's useful to know a few ankle and leg locks, should the situation require them.

We start the same way as with the fingers, with a passive exercise. Both partners are on the ground. Take the other person's foot and begin slowly working against the toes, then move up to the ankle. Explore the range of motion of all the joints. Notice how tension in the foot very quickly travels up into the knee and hip. Once you have a feel for this, move on to the next drill.

Both partners are on the ground and barefoot. A feeds in a slow attack to B. It can be a kick, it can be some kind of grab. B has to evade the attack and grab A's toe/s or foot, working to twist or lock the joint. Nice and slow to start, this is preparation work. From their, we can move on to some specific techniques.

Here is one way to get into a basic ankle lock. A is on the floor in guard position. B kneels and takes A's leg. One hand rests on the knee, the other circles under so that the forearm is supporting A's leg, close to the ankle.

From here B can either just lean back or sit. As they do, they rotate the locking hand forwards. This should have the effect of cutting the forearm into A's Achilles tendon. B's leg maintains a downward pressure to prevent A's knee from rising. Again, the power is in the leaning back and twisting

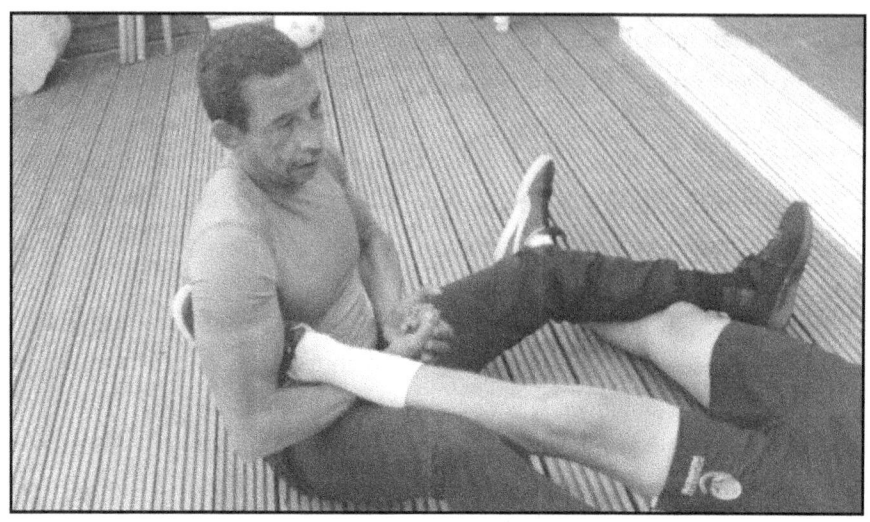

B simply swings their foot over A's leg and applies downward pressure.

For a basic heel hook, the locking arm goes under again, but in the opposite direction. A sits opposite B and grabs B's heel with their left hand, bringing it in tight against the body. B's right hand now goes over and

movement, not in applying tension.

There are numerous variations on this basic position. One option is for B to use a single arm to apply the lock and use their leg to check A's other leg as shown. It is also possible to lock the knee from this position.

clasps the left. The locking movement is achieved by rotating B's heel. Please be careful! Again, there are numerous variations, so play around with angles and positions.

The knee bar is a simple technique - after all the knee, like the elbow is a hinge joint. Again, this is usually a ground fighting technique but let's look at it from a different perspective.

A is on the ground and places one foot behind B's ankle and the other in front of the knee. Work to find the best position - I find just under the kneecap works best for me. A now pulls the ankle slightly forward while pressing in and down on the knee. This should lock the leg and cause B to fall. Again, work carefully and with minimal force to start, the knee can be fragile! As before, add in a slight rotation to make the movement more effective and work from different angles, too.

Of course, there are many ways of getting into these locks and many layers of refinement to add into them, particularly from a ground fighting perspective. For now, though, let's keep thing basic and start to work them in a moving environment. As before, A feeds in slow attacks to B, on the ground and B must respond by applying an foot or ankle lock. From there, work the lock flow drill in the same way as we did with the hands.

## ARM AND SHOULDER

We mentioned the arm bar a little already. Let's just go over some of the detail. The basic arm bar works on leverage. The most effective point to apply force is just above the elbow joint, not directly on it. As already described, we can increase its effectiveness by using rotational movements. Again,

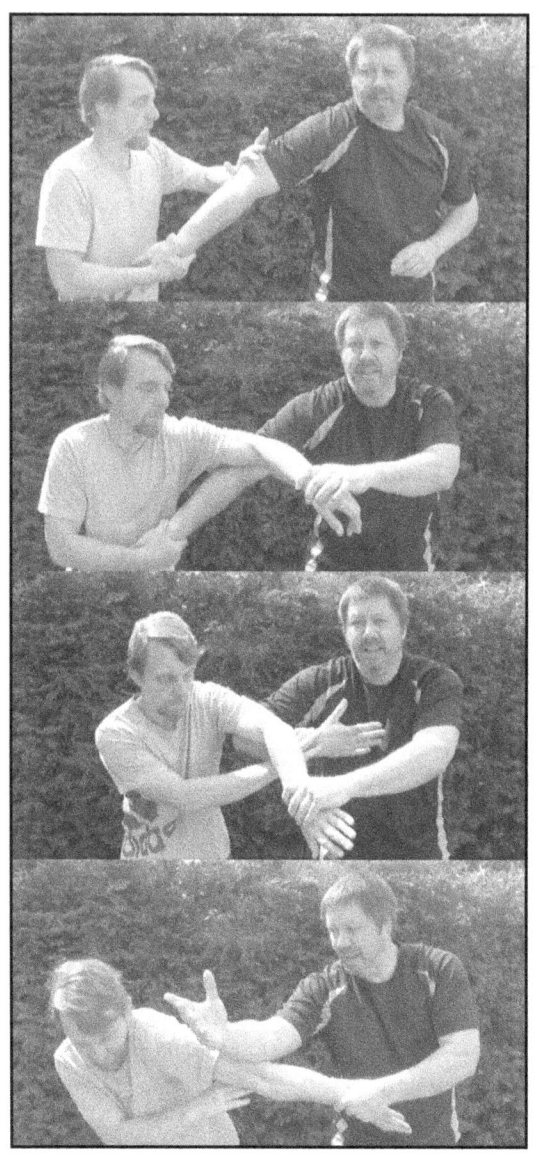

power comes through the movement, not through force. Another tip is to pull the opponent's wrist away from their body as you apply the lock. This should also have the effect of compromising their balance and can lead into throws and takedowns. Let's look at a simple flow drill that will help you get the hang of the technique.

A grabs B's right wrist with right hand . B steps back a little, rotating their right hand thumb upwards. As they do so, they apply the arm bar with left hand or forearm. Just apply light pressure for now but be sure the lock is on.

A slides their left hand down to grabbed arm to take B's left wrist and pull it forward and down.

A now pulls their right hand back pivoting their right forearm around the elbow. From there A now applies the arm bar to B. Repeat as required, flowing back and forth,slow at first on with just enough force.

Shoulder locks are good way of working into restraints and takedowns. Immobilising the shoulder locks most people up completely.

To work the basic technique, a stands in front of B. A now moves forward and a little to their left, bringing the left hand inside of B's right arm.

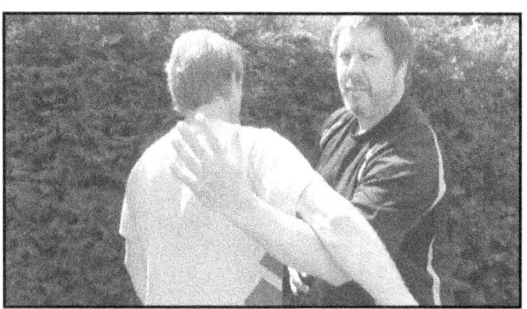

A's left hand snakes up and around onto B's shoulder as A steps round to face the same direction as B.

The trick to the next part is not to push on the shoulder, but to rotate it. A should push in slightly on the shoulder blade, then imagine they are lifting it up and forward. Work from the waist or with wave movement if you like. The movement should bend B forward, allowing A to move B around, or take them to the floor.

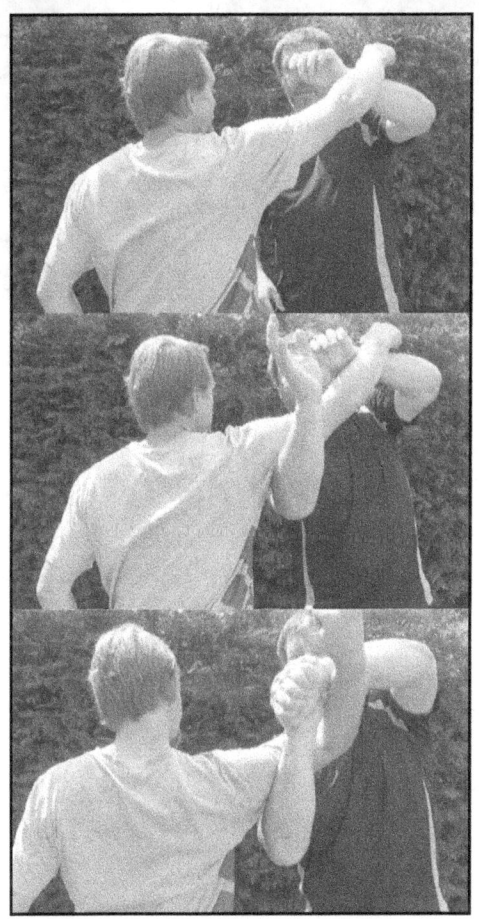

Another way to lock the shoulder is with a Figure 4 lock. For the basic set up, A feeds in a high line attack to B with their right hand. B rotates slightly to the left, bringing the left hand up to check the strike. B next threads their right hand under the attacking arm at the triceps. B now slides the checking hand forward and places it on the back of the left hand, so forming the figure 4. B can now feel how they can rotate and/or take a step forward in order to lock the shoulder into a takedown.

The last technique for the arm is the lifting lock. This involves twisting the arm in order to lock wrist, elbow and shoulder. As it brings

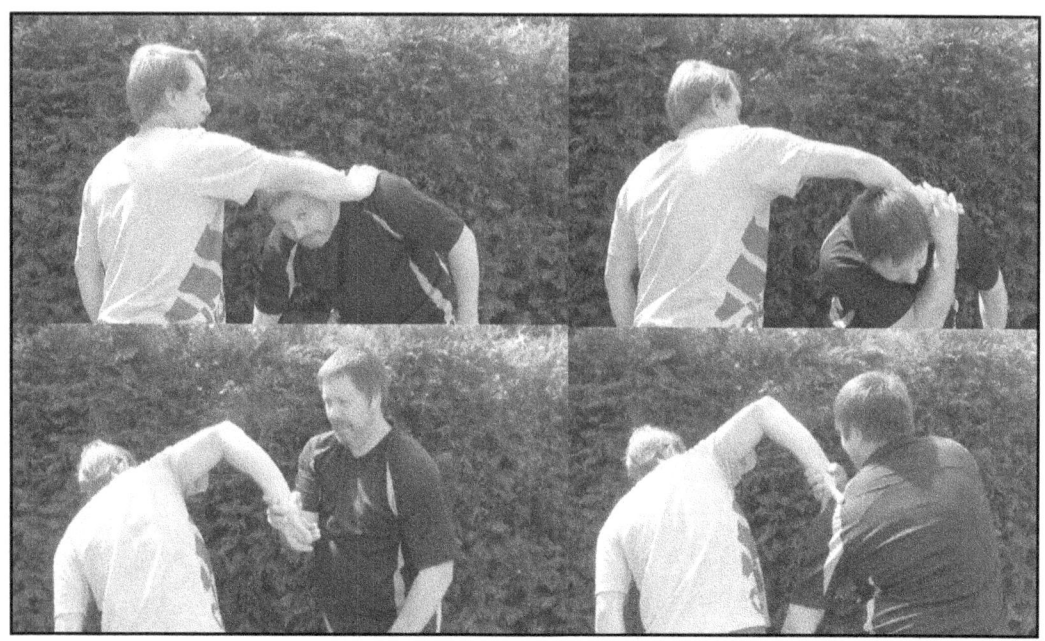

the attackers balance up on their toes, it is a good one for moving people around.

For our basic set up, A and B stand opposite each other. A places their right hand on B's left shoulder. B grabs A's wrist with their right hand and steps under and through the grabbing arm. As B straightens up, they twist and lift A's arm. The key is getting the right angle as you lift, as though your are pushing the arm back into the body. This should lock all three arm joints. Again, the power comes from the lifting of the body and the twist.

Run through each of this methods and once you can apply the basic technique smoothly, start to add in movement. Have A feed in slow strikes or grabs, B must position and apply one of the arm locks. In addition, change level every now and again to work against the knee. Don't feel you have to apply a "perfect" technique, remember the technique here is just to give you the feel and idea of the principles. Once you understand the principles, you will find numerous variations of these basic techniques, and become fluent at applying them in all types of position and situation.

## CHOKES

Chokes can be very useful, both to subdue an attacker by rendering them unconscious, and also as a way to pin or transport people. Of course, any work on the throat and airways must be carried out with all due care. In training, be aware of your partner's medical history - some people can be particularly sensitive to any work around the carotid sinus area, for example. This is one area where we will employ tapping out to

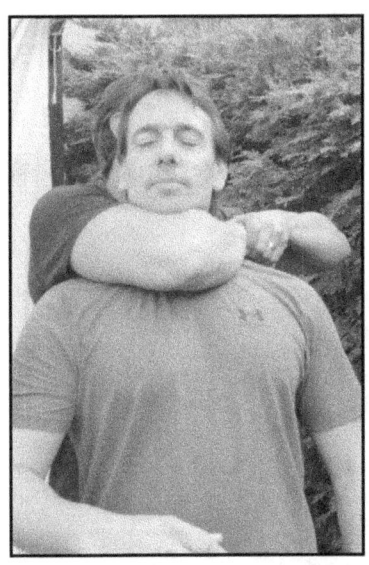

start with. A choke can come on surprisingly quickly, so if your partner taps, you should immediately release it.

I do not recommend choking people completely out, at least not at this stage. That is something that can be explored once people are experienced, but it should always be done only with the knowledge of how best to resuscitate people. Personally, I've never felt the need to routinely knock out students, whether with so-called "pressure point" strikes or through chokes. I feel any potential health risks outweigh whatever benefits there may be. However, in some training contexts, it may be appropriate to take a technique to its conclusion.

There are two types of choke - blood and air. We will show how these are applied with the arm but, of course, they can be put on with other parts of the body, too. As the names imply, the blood choke works by cutting the flow of blood to the brain, resulting in a shut down. The air choke works by sealing off the airway to the lungs. Both carry risks, though the air choke is potentially the most damaging, as it involves applying pressure directly to the trachea. The trachea, often called the windpipe, is a cartilaginous tube that connects the larynx to the bronchi of the lungs. As it is made of cartilage, the trachea is easy to damage. Think of it like a soft drinks can - it is easy to crumple in, less easy to pop it back out to its original shape. Always take care, then, when applying pressure directly across the throat.

For basic set up of each choke, we will have A sit behind B. For the blood choke, A passes a hand under B's chin and brings it round to clasp the opposite shoulder. Try to get B's chin to rest on the elbow. The aim now is to squeeze into the muscles at the side of then neck, in effect we are compressing one or both of

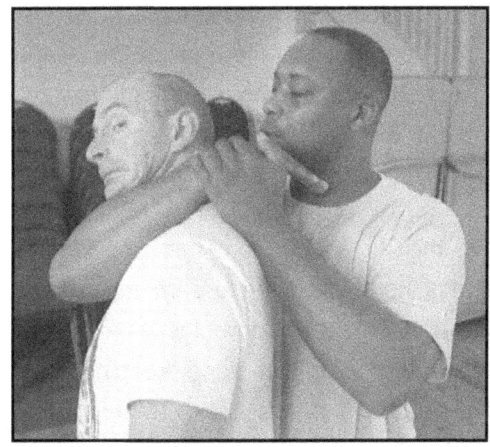

the carotid arteries and/or the jugular veins.

Try not to squeeze with tension, instead A should just move the hand towards their own neck and straighten the back a little. This squeezing and lift should have the desired effect. As B feels the choke begin to bite, they can tap. They say it takes 10-20 seconds to choke someone out using this method, but an expert can work it in much less time.

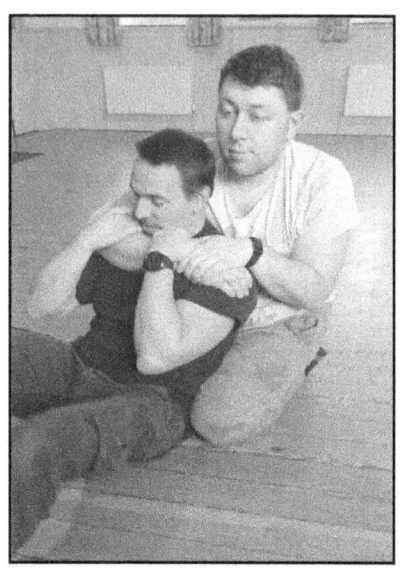

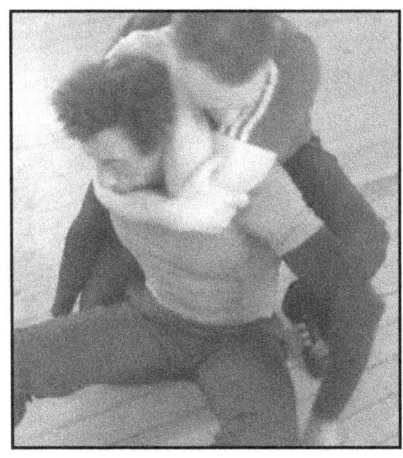

Of course, the main variation of this is the Sleeper Hold. From the same set up, A's other hand goes to the back of B's head. The choking hand comes across to rest on top off the rear arm's biceps. As you squeeze, push the head slightly forward.

For the air choke from this position, A brings the blade of the forearm across the front of B's throat. A now clasps the hands together to lock B in place, keeping their chest tight in to B's back. To apply the choke, A rotates the choking arm in and up, with a slight rotation. Please do this very carefully! The best way is to apply a little, then immediately release, do not keep the technique in fro more than a second or so.

For a variation, we will also look at a front choke. This uses the hand rather than the arm. All the usual cautions apply. A stands in front of B and places their hand on B's throat. For a simple hold, or to move B back,

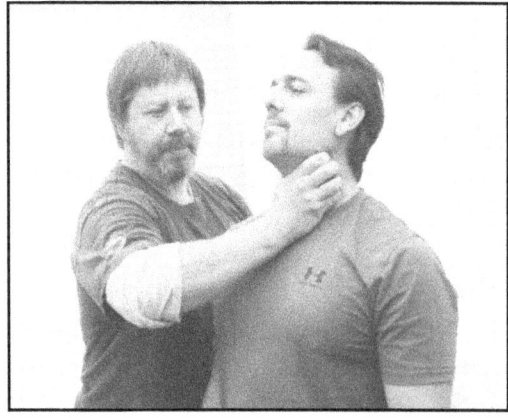

the grip can be quite wide. A pushes and lifts up slightly to move B. For an air choke, the grip is tighter. A curls their fingers into a C shape, hooking into the muscle at the side of the neck. The thumb hooks in to the side of the windpipe and pressure is applied. Again, please take great care with this technique, just apply for a second at this stage.

## LEARNING TO APPLY LOCKS

So, we have covered some basic positions and locks, largely against a static or slowly moving partner. I cannot stress how important it is to be fluid at this stage before moving on. If you are unable to apply a clean lock to a static partner, you will fare badly against movement and resistance. Always be aware of your position and how you are applying your force - these are the two key factors in getting lock to work.

The next stage is to have your partner come in with any type of attack. You evade and apply any of the above methods, or some variation as is appropriate. At this stage, I would still advise working at slow speed and maybe half level resistance from your partner. I'll speak more about resistance later on. Just be aware that if a lock is fully on and it is resisted, damage can result.

From there, run the same drill but in different positions. Start sitting in a chair, kneeling on the floor and so on. This will begin to develop your creativity and adaptability.

# CHAPTER FIVE
# TAKE DOWNS

From basic locks we will next move into take downs. I'm defining a take down here as a movement that gets a person to the floor while maintaining close distance to them. This is usually for the purpose of restraining a person in place but may also be to provide time to escape, to block the movement of a second attacker and so on.

Another aspect of take downs is in "friendly" work - usually in a close protection or bodyguarding context, whether professional or with family or friends. We will discuss this in more detail in later on but the basic principles are the same.

When practicing take downs with a partner, be sure that they are able to fall safely and manage any impact with the floor. We already mentioned a couple of Level Change exercises. Simply going to floor and standing back up again without using the hands is a good primer.

Consider this also, especially when training the basic take down methods. While partner A has the opportunity to work the take down, partner B has the opportunity to learn damage limitation - how to fall, how to deal with impact from the floor and, later on, how to escape or even counter-throw from these positions. When structured correctly, everyone should be learning form a Systema drill, not just be a dummy thrown around for one partner's benefit.

## STRUCTURE

The primary component of takedown work is body structure and bio-mechanics. We have already talked about simple machines. In that context, we can think of the body as a collection of hinges, levers etc, so it is those we will explore first

## THE SPINE

The spine forms the core of the body. It has a number of functions, both structural and in terms of relaying information. Any disruption to the spine will have a major effect on a person's stability, both physical and psychological. This is the main reason one of the Four Pillars is good form, which generally means a straight spine and level hips and shoulders. However, this should not be a fixed posture as there is no one such position that serves in all circumstances. For example, being upright and standing tall is good until there is incoming gunfire, when crouching or going prone may be more useful! In general, though, as we operate as bipeds, and our optimal posture or form is to have an upright spine and level hips and shoulders.

We can easily test this out. A stands in upright position. B pushes down on the shoulders or laterally into the body. An upright spine will handle the downward force easily. Think of the spine as a column of cotton reels. End to end, in line, they can withstand a lot of force. Likewise, as we have seen in our first drill, any lateral force

 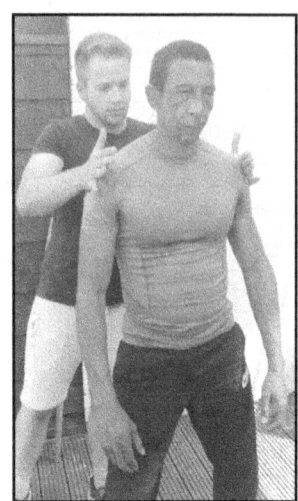

can be transmitted through the spine directly into the feet, so A can move away from the push.

Now repeat the same movements, this time asking A to bend the spine. Imagine now that one of those cotton reels is slightly out of alignment with the others. The structure becomes much weaker. You should find that the downward push collapses the body and the lateral push causes it to fold.

So how best to mis-align the spine? Think of three major hinges in the body - the neck, the hips and the knees. Applying force to any of these will affect the spine.

To learn how to do this, A stands close to B and now works with two hands. Start by placing one on the chest, one on the base of the spine. Push both hands inward, slowly, and see how the spine is disrupted. The top half of the body should be bent back over the hips. Next place a hand on the stomach and the rear of the head. Press with both and see how the body bends forward, again compromising spinal alignment.

Lastly, work against the knee. Place one hand on the chest and another hand (or leg) behind the knee. Press in once more, observing how the body is bent backwards. Take this principle and play with it, working all around the body. Think about the angles of force from your hands. You will find that your push is more effective if you "join" the hands together. In other words, the line of force coming from both hands should meet at some point. Pushing straight back on the right shoulder and straight forward on the left hip may turn

the person but will not take them down.

We already noted that lateral force in the body can be neutralised by moving the feet. This tells us that we need to prevent the leg moving to make a good takedown. To do this we block the hip or leg. Have A stand at the side of B, facing the opposite direction. A places their arm across B's upper chest and brings their hip into contact with B's hip. Now push forward with the upper arm while the hip moves back. B's upper body will be taken back and as the hip is blocked, B cannot step to neutralise the technique. Once the body is bent back, A can apply downward pressure to take B to the floor.

Once you have this principle, work around different parts of the body. Use one or two hands to push, one hand or another body part to block the hip or leg. For example, push on the back or pull the arm while placing one leg across the front of B's legs.

## BALANCE

The second major component of take down work is balance. As we mentioned in our *Systema Awareness* book, balance can be considered one of the "sixth senses." As long as a person is in balance, it is difficult to take them down or throw them. Again we can think of balance in both a physical and a psychological sense. I'm sure you've been thrown "off balance" mentally at some point - remember how that felt? In that moment, you were vulnerable. We will return to this concept later on. For now, let's start with some structural work and balance points.

A stands with feet shoulder width apart. B pushes in from the shoulder at the side. A may move a little but the position is quite stable. Now, picture a line between the feet that forms the base of triangle, front and back. The apex of the triangle is the balance point, the place at which A's balance is weakest. If B pushes on the chest or back towards one of those points, A will move easily.

Our next concept is centre of balance or centre of mass. Think of the pelvis as a bowl on which the body sits. If the bowl is tilted, the balance "spills out" over the edges. Likewise, if the upper body is pulled out of line, it can no longer sit comfortably in the bowl.

When standing, the centre of gravity is normally located in the abdomen at the level of the sacrum. In Oriental martial arts this place is usually referred to as the *hara* or the *dantien*. Stances tend to be sunk in order to keep all movements focused around the centre. But when we consider movement of the human body, things get more complicated. Every time we move an arm, a leg, change the position of the head, etc, the shape of our overall form changes. Carrying something heavy, like a suitcase, will also change our centre of gravity. In that sense our centre of gravity is a continually changing point in or outside the body that represents where the weight or mass of the rest of your body is equally balanced in every direction. Systema takes advantage of his by utilising a "floating" point of balance, but more on that later on. For the moment, let's stick with our basic centre of mass.

A stands in a comfortable position. B takes A's wrist and gently pulls the arm in different directions. See how far the arm has to be pulled before A's balance is effected. See also how different angles work in different ways. Pulling the hand straight up will have less effect than pulling to the side. Think back also to the triangle point - pull the hand towards the apex of the triangle. From the

placements, position and angles are correct, it should take very little effort to perform a take down. If we have to muscle through in order to achieve our goal we are likely not in the optimum position. Of course, there is nothing wrong with adding speed and force into our work but that should develop out of our precision, not be a substitute for it. Having worked our basics, let's next look at specific methods and some ways to refine our work.

## THE HEAD, DENSITY AND SPIRALS

"Where the head goes, the body follows" is a common martial arts saying. The easiest take downs are from the head, both because of the saying and because the head has plenty of "handles" for us to grab. To illustrate the first point, A stands on front of B and places a hand on B's forehead. A now same position, B now works directly against the hips. Push or tilt A's pelvis and see how it effects the equilibrium of the body.

So, we have three principles to begin working with - folding or collapsing the structure, blocking the legs and taking the balance. To begin working these, A feeds in a simple and slow grab to B. Allow the grab to just come on - not fully, but allow at least some contact. B shifts their body to protect it, places hands, hips, feet, etc in various positions on or around A and performs a gentle take down on them.

It should be gentle for two reasons - the first, at this stage, is to protect our training partner, especially if they are not so experienced in falling. The second is to help us to monitor our tension levels. If our

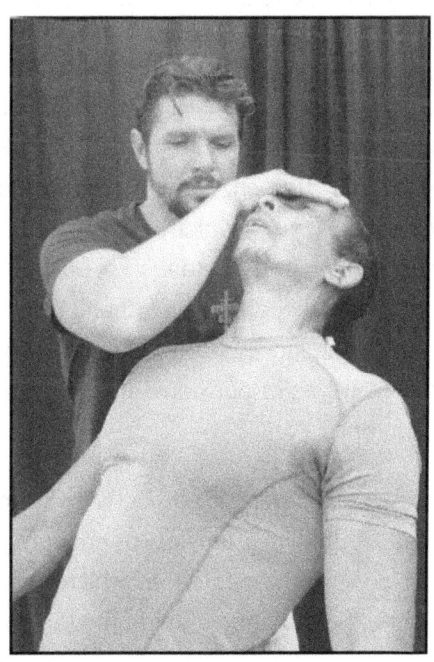

gently pushes back. The aim is to kink the neck, so taking the weight of the head over the balance point. Once the head is tilted, B pushes down into the spine. When done correctly, this will collapse the spine straight down. If necessary, A can block the hip as before.

This technique uses a few principles. We see the use of the hinge and balance, but it also uses the idea of density. We can think of density as tension in the body. You can feel this yourself by doing the above movement. Tilt your head back, you will feel a slight tension in the neck and perhaps the shoulders. This tension is a natural response by the nervous system to protect the body. The spine is in a vulnerable position, so the muscles tense to protect it. However this tension makes it difficult to neutralise any incoming force.

When you are in that position, any downward pressure on the head is transmitted into the neck and gets "stuck" there. It only has one way to go and that is down the spine, which causes further misalignment and so leads to our take down. If a body part is relaxed and free to move, incoming force can usually be "waved out" as in our usual pushing and striking drills.

However, if a person is particularly strong, it may be that this tension is enough to resist our incoming force. In which case, we should add in some spiral movement.

We already established that the body finds it difficult to resist force in more than one direction. So try the same exercise again but this time, as A presses (gently) down, the also rotate B's head slightly. The direction doesn't matter, the point is we are applying a torque into the neck, making the movement virtually impossible to resist, particularly when done at speed - but don't try this just yet! Get the feel of this movement, again the positions and angles, then move on to the next drill.

A and B now stand some distance apart and

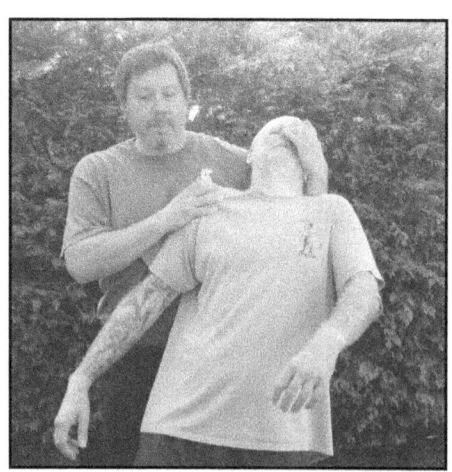

slowly walk towards each other. As they get close, A applies the takedown above to B and continues walking. B gets up, turns and the drill repeats, this time with B performing the take down on A. This gets you used to movement, plus also feel how you can put the momentum from your walk into the take down.

Let's move onto those handles! Our first technique was rolling. But there are plenty of ways we can grab the head and use the place we grab to control its movement - the ears, the nose, the chin and so on. A moves around B and, in each new position applies a gentle grab and twist to B's head / face. So, grab the ears, hook the fingers in to the side of the nose, use the hair, place the palm over the chin, you get the idea. You don't have to go into takedowns yet, just get the feel of rolling and manipulating the head through its handles. Your movement should be smooth and sensitive, again we are looking to apply this work with as little warning to the opponent as possible.

Think back to our preparation drill with the ball. Spend some time rolling it around in your hands and forearms. Don't stand on the spot, walk around as you roll. Feel how the angle of your arms change, but the ball should always be under control.

For stage two, A now throws the ball at B's face. B should move aside slightly, catch the ball and immediately go into the rolling movement above.

Once you can do that smoothly, put the ball down and have A feed in a slow punch. B should evade this, as they did the ball, and get

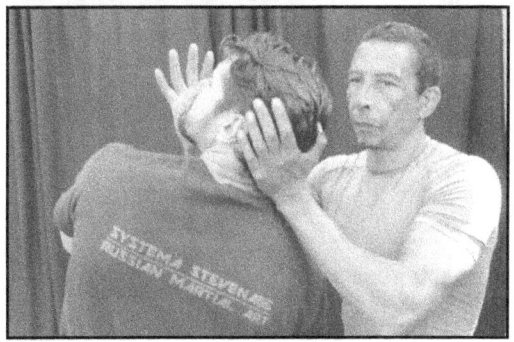

hold of A's head. Use the same movement, plus handles, to control A's head. You can either play around a little, or work straight into a take down - in which case you may also need to block the hips.

A nice method that uses the leverage of the arm, head control and a spiral, works like this. To practice the basic set up, A stands in front of B and places their right hand under B's left wrist. A now lifts the hand, bringing B's arm up high. A's left hand wraps around the side of B's head. Use the leverage of the lifting arm to bring B's head down and to the side. A should use a spiraling movement to assist in this movement.

A should imagine they are bringing B's head in towards their own navel. At the same time, A continues lifting B's arm up and over. This action should twists B's whole body. If A steps back, B should fall in front of them. Once you have the basic methods, work at getting into it from different positions, against a grab, a punch and so on.

We mentioned arms in the last drill but we can also use other parts of the body to control the head. You can work the same exercise with the ball but this time gather it into the chest. One hand keeps the chest pinned to the body and you rotate it by waving or rolling the chest. This method has the advantage of keeping one hand free.

We can use the body in other ways, too. Let's say we have grabbed the ears (we will

be looking at ways to grab later on.) We can pull with the hands but a more effective and efficient method is to rotate from our body - this could be the shoulders, the hips, or by stepping. For the hands, imagine you are turning a big steering wheel - the power is in the movement, not the tension.

Let's look at some other specific movements we can work with the head. Staying with the ears, here's a good take down from the rear - so perhaps in a situation where you have a friend in trouble. A approaches B from behind and places the tips of their first two fingers inside and at the top of B's ears. A now presses in rotates up and then back and down - making a small circle with the hands. When done correctly, this will "float" B's head up , allowing A to bring it back and down as in our very first technique. Once the body is misaligned, guide the head carefully down to the floor.

Another good method from this position is to work against the eyes. From the back, A brings their hands over the shoulders and round to gently but smartly tap on B's eyes. Please check with your partner first in case they have contact lenses or some other issue! A short, sharp tap is all that is required, this will be enough to make B flinch and jerk their head back, breaking the

alignment of the neck. Once B does this, A should press quickly down on B's shoulders to effect the take down. This is a very effective move but please practice it carefully!

Pulling hair was mentioned earlier. That can also be done from the back, or from the sides or front - assuming the person has hair to grab! But there is a specific way we should grab, for maximum effect.

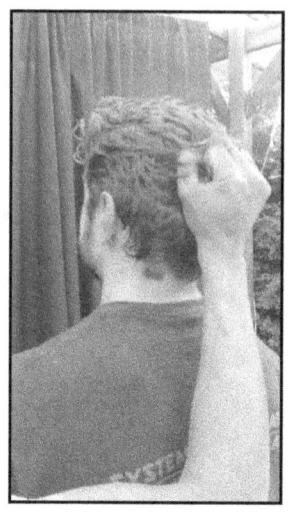

The usual method is to grab the hair by bring the hand straight down onto the head and closing the fingers. Instead, place the the hand on the head, then slide the fingers into the hair. This gives you a much deeper grab and, so, more control.

Earlier we spoke about a strong person using tension to resist our movement. If we are working to bend the neck, there is a useful tip to overcome this. Let's say A has their hand on B's face and is trying to push the head back. B is strong and resists. What A can do is to remove B's tension by sharply rubbing their palm across the tip of B's nose. Imagine you are vigorously wiping something as though trying to clean it! There should be some downward pressure too. This will cause B to flinch and the neck will relax, allowing A to complete their technique.

Before we move on to the rest of the body I just want to mention footwork. Although for take downs we want to keep a person close, there must also be a space for them to fall in. Consider the position below. We can see that A is trying to take B down with an arm bar into the space they are already occupying. Instead, A should step back, thereby creating the hole or space for B to fall into. Of course we also use footwork as

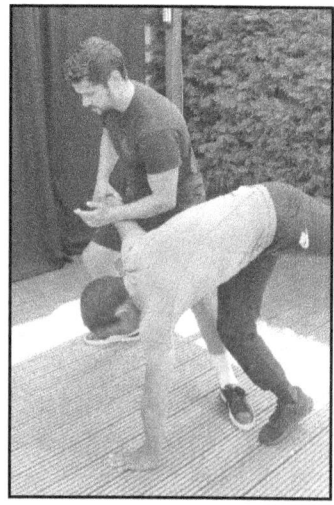

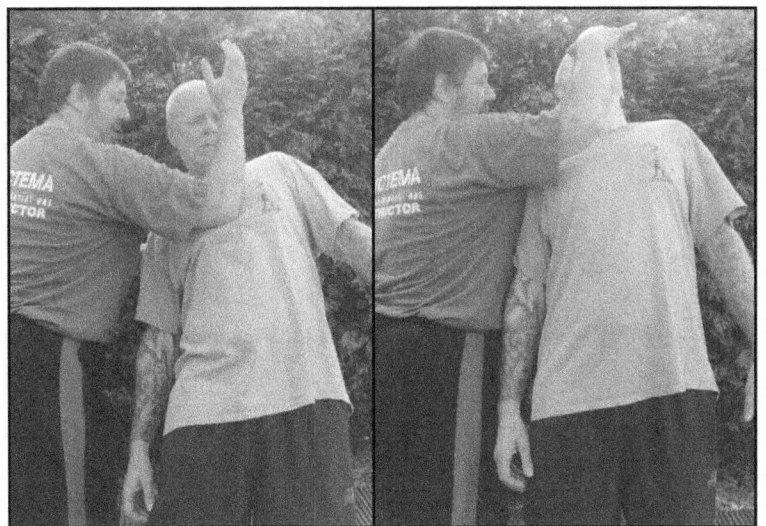

a force magnifier, especially when it comes to rotation movements. So another tip, if you are struggling to take some one down, is to check your feet.

the body is tilted but it may be difficult to get sufficient downward force from the hand. A rotates their upper elbow down into B's chest and drops their weight down through it. Don't push, use the body weight to do the work - spine straight and sink!. So here we have an example of a structure break, an applied spiral, density in the chest and use of our own strong posture to power the technique.

## THE BODY

The torso is the densest part of the body. We can think of it like a big wardrobe. How do we move such a heavy item of furniture? We tilt it, up onto one corner, then it can be pivoted with ease. If we think of the hips and shoulders as corners, we begin to see how we can work with the body. Think back to our earlier exercise, where we were placing two hands on the body and pushing. Run those again, working the opposite corners. One hand pushes the right shoulder back, the other the left hip forward, for example.

This should twist the body but won't necessarily push it down. This is where our spiral movement comes into play. So A is performing the move as above. See how

## THE ARMS

The arms obviously give us a good lever to work with against the body. If we go back to our basic arm bar, we can see that extending the movement out, usually by taking a step out to the side, will take our partner to the floor - face first, so be careful in training. The same applies to the shoulder lock, simply extend the movement out to take the person down

We should just discuss level change here. At first, people often bend over in order to take their partner to the floor. This breaks good form and also leaves us vulnerable to a counter-throw or to other opponents. The best way to put body power into a takedown is either to squat, keeping good form, or to change level. Let's take the arm bar as an

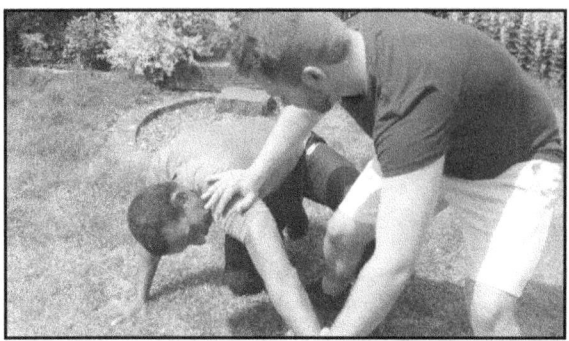

example. In the first picture above, A bends in order to effect the take down. See, instead, how in the second picture A goes into a semi-squat position to achieve the same result. This will not only make for a stronger technique, it allows A more control of B and also to remain alert for other attacks.

The arm gives us good leverage but we can also work take downs from the hand and wrist. One works along the same lines as our basic Gooseneck hold. A approaches B from any angle. With their nearest hand, A takes and lifts B's nearest hand. A now places their other hand on the top of B's wrist, bending the hand down into our triangle shape mentioned before.

The pressure should be directed down the arm, through the elbow and straight into the ground. Done firmly and correctly this will cause B to fall straight down, due to the tension caused by the wrist lock.

An even more basic method is to pull sharply down on the wrist. In this case, A approaches from the rear, grabs B's wrist in both hands and pulls sharply down - imagine you are ringing a bell! To increase effectiveness, pull the arm out away from the body to tip the balance.

Any twisting movement of the wrist, such as in our earlier anti-grab techniques, can be naturally concluded as a take down. Again,

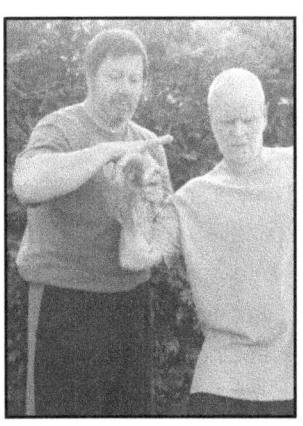
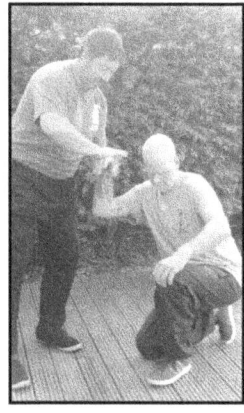

check your footwork, make sure to create that space for your partner to fall into. You may even be able to work the same from the finger, given the right angle of pressure.

Another nice technique uses the elbow to break structure. To get a feel for how this works, have A grab B by the wrist. B now pulls their hand back, by turning or stepping, in order to stretch out A's arm a little and to effect their balance. B's free hand now moves to inside A's elbow. Note how the "mouth" of the hand fits into the elbow crease. From here, B circles that hand out and down in a smooth movement. This, combined with the forward stretch of the arm, will pull A out of their stance and then guide them down.

The same method can be applied to a chest grab or, with practice and good

position, before the attacked hand has even made contact. You can also experiment with using the edge of the hand to "chop" into the attacking elbow.

SINGLE AND DOUBLE LEG

Leg takedowns can be a very powerful move, as anyone who has played rugby will know! There are a few ways to do this, we will look at two version of the single leg and also the basic double leg take down for now. In order to practice, we can first start from a kneeling position

A kneels in front of B. A curves their arm around B's lead leg and pulls it towards them. At the same time, they move the same shoulder forward to press against B's knee or higher. The idea is to lift the foot and push the knee back, moving the bodyweight through. This should make A fall backwards. A kneels in front of B. A wraps both arms

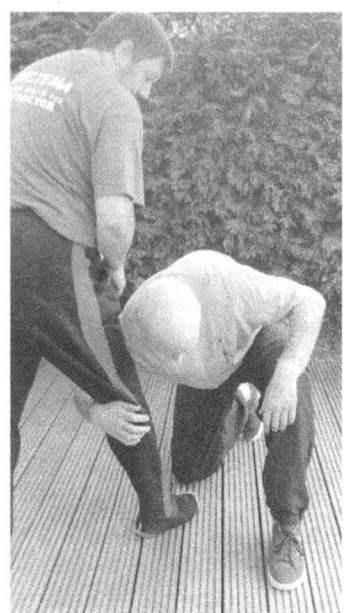 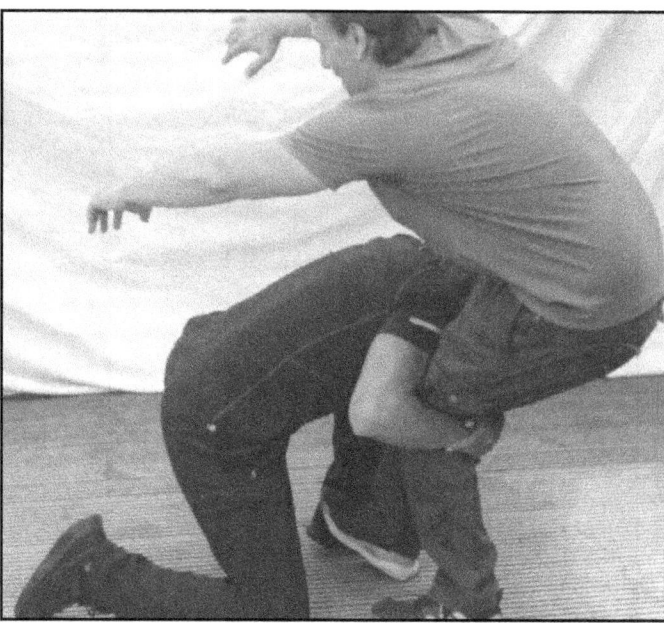

around B's lead leg. They now roll to their side - if they have B's left leg, A rolls to the right. To perform the roll, A can practice by sitting into B's stance and falling to their right. A should be sure to lift B over them as they fall.

To perform a double leg, from the same position, A wraps an arm around each of B's leg and presses forward with the shoulder. They can also lift B a little as they push forward.

Once you have the positioning right, you can work into the same movement from a standing position. I suggest starting from a neutral standing position and gradually adding in more movement. The key is timing and position, of course, once again when done correctly there should be very little effort involved. Think about where the other person's balance point is, be sure to co-ordinate the leg left with the forward pressure. Take care not to lift the leg right into your own groin! Also be sure when lifting another person, even if only for a short time, that you have good posture. Try and get your hips under the lift and push up from your legs. Remember that any faults in your structure may not only make you weak but also give an opponent an opportunity to counter.

We will finish this section with a slightly more unusual version of this technique, a roll into a single leg take down. We will start from kneeling again.

A kneels in front of B, slightly to one side. A wraps an arm around B's leg, in this case right arm to right leg. The arm should be pulled in quite tight. A now performs a roll,

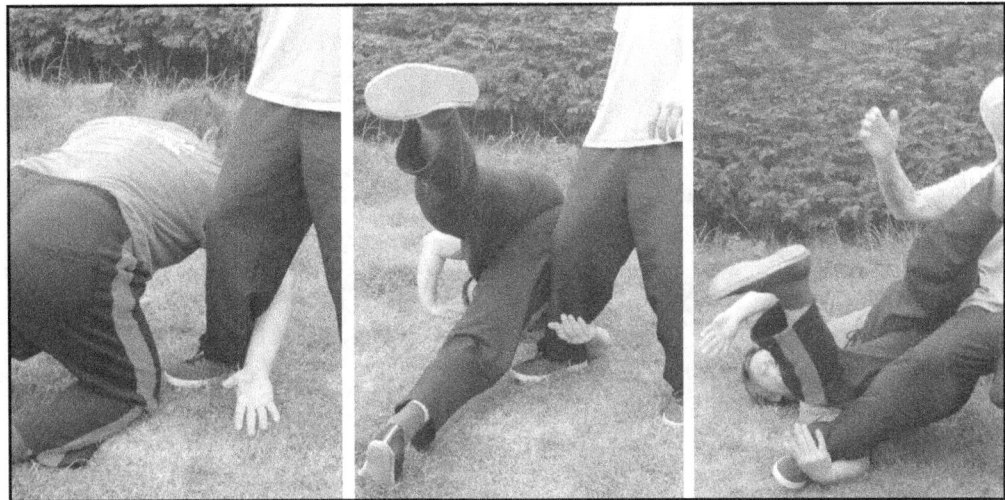

over the right shoulder. As A rolls they flick the legs up and across B's body (B should have a hand in place to protect their face). A's butt rolls up and across B's leg. The combination of this, B's foot being pinned in place and the legs going across the body should make B fall.

Be very careful when you try this not to roll your weight onto B's knee. In practice, it might be best once B is moving to release their foot. In use, you can roll across the knee to damage it.

Once you have the movement down, you can also work from standing. Once again, start from a neutral position and work in more and more movement. For the "full" version A moves in quickly towards B, makes a distracting movement up high with the hands, then dives into the roll, taking B's leg as they go. Please exercise care when working at speed!

## THE KNEES

We have seen already how the knee is a vulnerable joint and so a good target for structure breaking. Let's look at working against it with hands and feet.

A sits or kneels in front of B. A begins gentle work against the knee with one or both

hands. For example, have B bring one foot forward. A now presses just under the kneecap with the edge or inside of their hand. Feel for the right angle in order to lock the knee - think in and a little down. With the correct direction and use of force, B will fall.

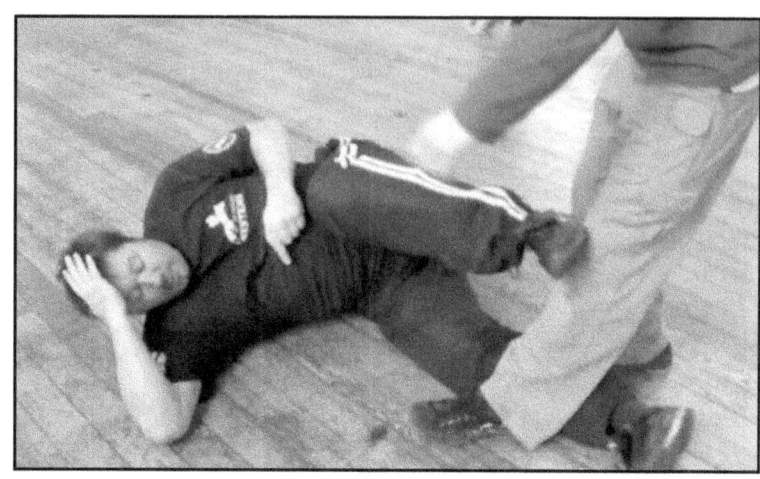

Explore similar work against the side and rear of the knee. A good tip when working against the knee is to think of that rotation or spiral principle again. For example, in the above method you might find that if B is in a very strong stance, their leg will not move. In this case, add a slight rotation into your push. Move slightly out to the side, then forward and down, that should do the trick. The same applies if working to the side or rear - add in a little rotation for extra effect, always taking care of your partner, of course.

Once you have a feel for that, A now lays on the floor with B above them. A applies the same work, but using their feet rather than hands. See how you can hook one foot in behind B's ankle and use the other to press against the knee, for example. Remember the rotation and remember to apply force through movement, not through tension.

Next, apply the same work against the ankle. As the ankle is a smaller and more flexible joint, this calls for more precision but is a great take down when done right. Start by sitting again and using your hands to lock the joint. Use a rotation to get into the joint, pressing down once it is turned a little. The trick here is to keep B's foot pinned to the floor. If they can lift the foot, the lock will be neutralised. Working to the sides is best,

from the inside or the outside.

From there, both partners stand and A applies the same work to B's ankle but with their feet. Again, this calls for precision. Place the ball of your foot on the outside of B's ankle, just on the large bone. Now imagine you are pressing down an accelerator pedal, that forward and down movement. This will once more lock the ankle and cause B to fall if done correctly.

We remain standing for the next exercise. This is learning how to lock the knee with your own knee. There are three basic positions, front, inside and outside. The key, again, is to fix the foot in place. We can do this by "hooking in" with our own foot, as follows.

A stands with one foot forward. B places their own foot in the positions above, in turn. In each position, B hooks around A's foot, then applies gentle pressure against A's knee with their own. Remember the rotation! Sideways, forward, down. B should apply pressure by rotating their hip and sinking, not with tension from the leg. Work each position until you can move smoothly into each and apply the take down.

If working the knee from the back, it can be buckled but not so much locked. However, this can still help us in a take down, such as in one of our previous applications. So when, A stands at B's side and places their right hand across the body to push the shoulder down and back, A's right leg can not only block B's hip, A can use their right foot to push into the back of B's knee, so buckling the leg.

We can also work directly from the front. To lock the knee from a standing position, A stands on B's foot, then squats a little, so pressing knee against knee. Add in a little rotation for full effect and please exercise caution.

Here's a professional takedown that works against the leg. It is very effective when done correctly but is also potentially damaging, so please practice with care. This works from a rear approach. B stands and A moves in from the back. When in range, A sharply strikes up with their knee into the back of B's thigh. If you feel with your fingers you will find a nerve point in the centre of the muscle. This will help the technique but is not vital.

If the strike is administered correctly, B's knee will naturally lift up in a flinch. This has the effect of raising the heel. A now uses the downward movement of their striking leg to step or stamp down on B's vulnerable ankle. Add a little rotation to the movement. If the toes are touching the floor, the foot will be locked in place and B will either fall or take damage to the ankle. Again, please practice this carefully, nice and slow to start!

Of course, we can also work against the knees with our feet from standing. A walks towards B. At the right point, B presses into A's knee with a foot. As well as precision of placement there is a question of timing here, too. The optimum time to apply the push is just as A's heel hits the ground. The foot is committed, the weight is just coming forward into it. Applying before or after this point may mean that A can change the position of there leg and step away from the force. To get the feel of this, you could go back with working hands

against walking knees from a sitting position first. We generally have more control over our hands than feet, so this a safer way to learn the timing and angles.

Our last method also calls for good timing. This is the foot sweep and again, when done correctly, is devastating. No matter how strong a person is, if you take away their point of support, they will fall. This also has the advantage of being "invisible" work, very difficult to see it coming. It works a treat against queue jumpers - no, don't do that!  To practice the method, A and B walk side by side. Nice and steady. A aims to match B's pace, step for step. Get into the rhythm and length of stride. Once matching it. A now tries to apply the sweep. The timing is similar to before. Just as B's stepping foot touches the ground, A should gently sweep it away. If B's weight is committed, they will at least stumble, or even fall.

The other timing option is for A to occupy the space that B is about to step into. So this is a little earlier, A places their foot in the exact spot as B commits to the step. Unless B is very quick, they will reflexively move their foot away, so losing balance again. In my experience this is a very common technique used by cats, particular when you are coming down the stairs carrying something heavy!

The method requires practice to get the timing right but, once you have it, start working from different positions. A and B approach, A follows B, A sweeps in from the side, and so on. You could also have B moving into apply a strike or grab. Another option is to apply the sweep from a grab.

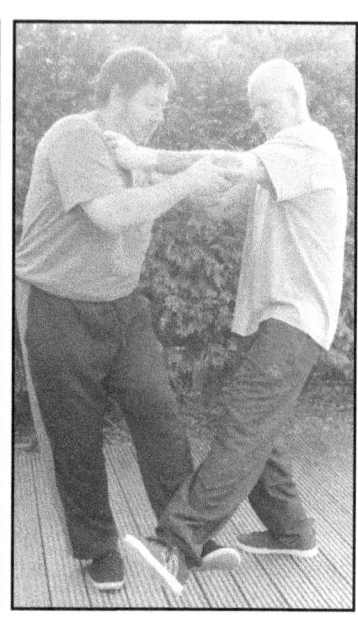

You can practice that with this exercise. B grabs A. Nothing fancy to start, a chest grab will do. Now, consider this. If A can control B's body movement, they will know exactly where and when B will step. So from this position, A rotates their shoulders back and takes a slight step with it. This will pull B's body forward, so they will naturally step out to keep balance. This will make it easy for A to apply the sweep.

When you stat working sweeps, you will find yourself looking down a lot. This is fine, it helps us get timing and position. Eventually, though, we want to be able to play this work by feel or with peripheral vision. When in contact with a person, we should always have the feel of where their centre of balance and feet are - more about that later. As far as vision goes, here's a method we use to develop awareness of foot position without looking down.

A and B stand opposite each other. A has to stand on B's foot, B has to avoid. Both should try and keep their eye line up, in normal position. For variations work with and without contact. Once both have had a

go, make it freestyle, either partner can step. You can add in the sweeps too. For full effect, have a group of people work the drill, say five or six. After a time you will get a good visual sense of where people's feet are by watching their shoulders. It's also worth putting some time into watching how people walk - you can learn a lot about a person by how they walk!

COMBINATIONS

So now we have some ideas on using individual body parts for take downs. But there is nothing to see we cannot combine this parts, in fact we should! Let's run through some examples.

A comes in to grab B's lapel. B uses the inside elbow hook to pull A in closer, from where they can wrap A's head with their other hand. From here, A rotates out using a shoulder wave. A simple squat and B is taken to the floor.

A walks to B in a threatening way. B kicks out to A's knee, locking it and so bringing A's head forward. B grabs A's ears and rotates, taking B to the floor.

A swings a hook punch to B. B circles inside the movement, checking it with their rear hand. B's front hand slides under A's chin as they step behind to block the hip. B lifts, rotates and presses the chin down to take B to the floor.

A has B pinned against a wall. B presses and rotates into A's knee. This disrupts A's structure and brings B's head forward. From

there, A controls and rotates into a take down.

These are simple examples, the combinations are endless. So, to finish, we will work two things. First, run through all the examples above, applying a single method against a partner feeding in slow attacks. Second, once you have the timing to work against movement, begin to chain your techniques together as outlined above.

Work from grabs, punches, walking, anything you like. At this stage we are still working "nicely." This is the learning phase, not the testing phase. We will talk about speed and resistance later on, first we need to be able to apply our work under little or no pressure!

**COUNTER TAKE DOWNS**

When you are fluent in regular take downs, start working counters into your training. This is where we reverse a take down and we can apply it at three different stages.

FLOOR

In this case we work at the end of the take down. So our partner applies the take down (from our grab, punch etc). We are taken down to the floor, from where we apply our own take down. Think back to the work we did against the legs for ideas. For example, A pushes B down to the floor. B hooks an arm around a's leg and pushes the body into A's knee for the take down, so taking them down. Of course, if your are feet closer to A you can use them hook and push A's knees.

## HALF WAY

This time we act as the take down is underway. For example, A grabs B round the neck and tries to take them down. B keeps their spine straight but goes with the movement a little. B uses the squat to push into A's knee and so collapses their structure.

## AS IT STARTS

In this case, B reacts as soon as they feel the take down coming on. For example, A grabs B around the neck. Before A can begin their take down, B responds, using the grabbing arm as a lever. B pivots and drops their weight, using a hand to the opposite shoulder for added effect.

You can run each of these as drills, with partners swapping roles each time. Keep things simple to start, working into deeper grabs as you progress. The aim of these exercises is to be sensitive to your partner's movement, structure and tension. Learn to respond to or to pre-empt movement by feeling, not by sight. If in close contact with a person, you should be aware of where their feet are and where their point of balance is purely through touch.

Take the time to develop these skills as they really come into play later on when we move into internal work.

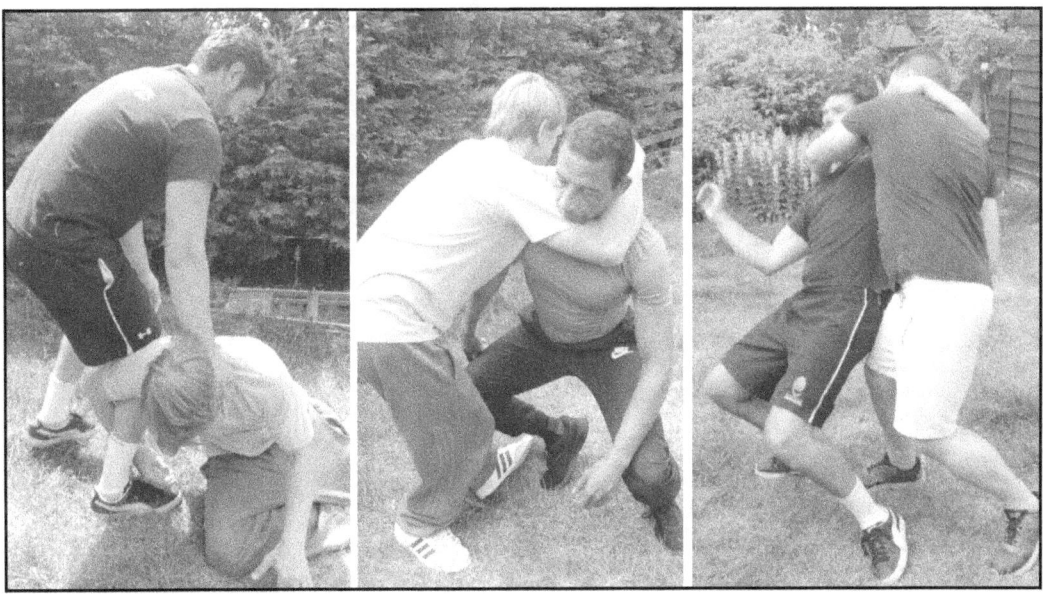

# CHAPTER SIX
# THROWS

Take downs have a major vertical component - we are usually collapsing a person into their own base, in much the same way a tower block gets demolished. Knock out the foundations, break the structure in the right places, and the building collapses into itself. Throws introduce a horizontal element into the process. Generally, we throw a person away from us, usually to the floor, sometimes into something. This adds in an extra layer of potential impact and damage, of course. I've heard before of even a basic throw being described as "hitting someone with the planet." Gravity does its job, with a little assistance, the ground does the rest. In a similar way, we could also described the affect of a throw as SDS - Sudden Deceleration Syndrome. The damage is caused by the impact, though we can add additional damage in too, should we need to.

The first requirement of training throws with a partner is that everyone can fall safely. As I mentioned before, this is a big subject in itself, something that should be addressed in your basic training. Here are a few ideas, though, to help develop good impact control. These exercises are a progression from the Take Down preparation work, so make sure you can do those first. Work a forward fall by using a waist high obstacle. Allow your body to fold over it, let yourself relax and go into the fall. Alternatively, find something you can lay on and slide / fall off of. From here, work to leap or dive over an obstacle. Feel free to use mats at first, then progress onto harder surfaces.

If working with a partner, to start A gently leads partner B into falls. For example, A stands in front and takes B's wrist. A blocks B's legs and pulls them forward, leading them into a diving fall and roll. This works the same way as the take down methods from last chapter - one partner is learning the mechanics of a throw, the other the means to cope with it.

Once people have a good grip on falling, you can try a more challenging exercise. Best to practice on a soft surface to start and not throw too high to begin with. Four people grab a limb on A. They pick A up, as though

they were going to give the person "the bumps". A is now swung back and forth. At the high point on the third swing, everyone lets go, so throwing A through the air. Remember swing low first, pick up height only when A is comfortable to do so.

In mechanical terms, then, our throws work in much the same way as our take downs - with that added horizontal aspect. If we go back to our basic arm bar, we have already seen it as a lock and as a take down. Repeat the take down version but this time add in a much longer pulling movement on the arm. The aim should be to pull the person completely off of their feet, so that their body goes parallel to the floor. Blocking the hips will usually help.

Throws can be broadly divided into four types. Lifting, leverage, body weight, scissors. There is also what we might call the empty throw, which we will discuss later on. Again, rather than list a ton of throwing techniques, which would fill the rest of the book, we will look at some basic examples of each of the above, then discuss how we can work those principles into our throws.

## LIFTING

In its simplest terms, we lift someone up above our head and throw them across the room, Incredible Hulk style! You need good position, timing and structure for this and it can be devastating. To practice. A walks to B, places a foot between A's feet, and grabs B at hip and collar. The grip can be adjusted to other vulnerable areas. The main thing is we have points of contact low and high. A's momentum should cause them to tip forward. As they do so, B straightens up, so lifting A using the power of the legs and the momentum. From there, execute the throw. For a variation of the above, B squats in and forward as A walks in, grabbing A's wrist with one hand and placing their shoulder into A's groin. From there, B pulls the wrist back while scooping with the shoulder and standing up into what is known as a Fireman's Carry.

Another throw that uses lifting is the good old standard shoulder throw. A stands before B, then steps in, grabs B's arm with both hands, one high one low. As they do this, A rotates, bringing their back in close to B's body. A now bends and lifts, taking B over the shoulder and into the throw. Again, this is about position and timing, not force and tension. The best throws look and feel effortless, they can appear deceptively easy to the untrained eye. And, of course, as the saying goes "the greater the master, the less you see!"

One other aspect of lifting throws is for friendly work. We mentioned this in context of take downs, but the same applies here too. We may have to lift and carry an injured or unconscious person, for example. Practicing lifts into throws teaches us some good ways to do this,

## LEVERAGE

We already discussed the arm bar as a throw, here is a variation that also use the arm as a lever. The set up is a little similar to the shoulder throw, but there is less body contact.

A grabs B by the wrist. B returns the grab and lifts A's hand. B's other hand cups A's elbow. B now turns, extend A's arm out straight. Be careful as you practice the next part. B lifts the elbow and presses down a little on a's hand. B now steps as they finish the turn. The throw is a casting movement, similar to what you would do with a fishing rod. To add in extra power, put in a shoulder wave. Project the lifting hand up and out as the pressing hand goes sharply down. Again, the power is in the movement, not in applying force.

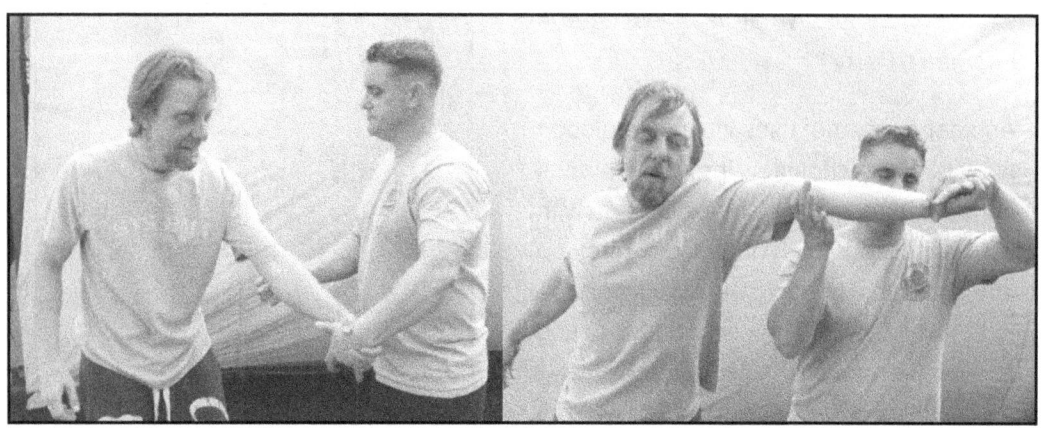

## BODY WEIGHT

Also known as sacrifice throws, this is where we use our falling body weight to throw our opponent. The most commonly known are the stomach throw and the dropping shoulder throw

A stands opposite B and grabs their lapels. A now sits, placing a foot into B's stomach or leg. A rolls back, lifting B up and over into the throw. If you want to work with a little momentum, have B walking into A. This can be just a throw, or A can continue their roll to finish astride B's chest.

A stands opposite B and reaches out to grab. B brings their right hand under A's right arm and grabs the sleeve. B now turns 180 degrees and drops to their knees so throwing A over the shoulder.

In both cases the drop of the bodyweight is what powers the throw, meaning of course that we must be able to connect our body weight to our partner. If a person has a strong grab on us, this is not normally a problem, though our level change should be quick or the person may just let go! If you have to grab the other person to throw them, think about our earlier leverage. An arm is

a good choice as we can pull it away from the centre of balance for increased leverage. Also, always be sure to take the person over you rather than just pulling them down on top of you. Control of the arm will help, you can also use a knee or foot to guide their trajectory.

Work the principle from different positions. For example, A grabs B from the side. B returns the grab and sits, bringing A over them to the floor.

Sacrifice throws generally work in an arc - we are taking the person up and over us but we can also drop our weight into a person. A grabs B from the rear. B quickly drops their weight back into A's knee - take care when practicing not to lock the knee. B should be sitting back towards A's rear triangle point.

The other aspect of sacrifice throws is that you will end up on the ground - so be sure that you have some abilities for ground movement, ground fighting, or the ability to get up quickly.

## SCISSORS

This is the concept of applying force in two opposing directions in order to throw a person. The most basic version of this is the clothesline throw.

A walks quickly to B. At the last moment, B moves outside but leaves their arm outstretched. The arm contacts A across the upper chest, then rotates forward and down. So we are using the momentum of the hips and legs moving forward against the upper body being pushed back. It should be simple to take A down this way.

Another version is to also apply pressure against the legs. Have A feed in a punch or grab to B. B ducks under and moves into the space below the attacking arm. Let the head or hand lead this movement. B steps forward, bringing their leg into contact with A's right leg, particularly the knee. B now straightens the body, pressing forward with the leg as the arm / elbow pushes back into A's body. The movement should pitch A forwards.

These are our main throwing principles, then. Though we separate out for clarity in training, the reality is all of these one or more of these principles may be used at any time. The shoulder throw uses a lift, for example, but adding a body drop at the start with help with the throw. Another example is a scissors throw that uses bodyweight.

To practice this, A holds B's leg. B now turns and drops their hands down towards the supporting foot. That foot goes up behind A. B drops into the hands, at the same time twisting the waist. It is important to work with power of the hips rather than just trying to push with the legs. The combination of weight drop, twist and scissors will bring A down.

Work through each of these basic methods and once again think of them not as techniques but as principles. Then we can start working them in a more freestyle environment.

## TRAINING THROWS

The stick is a great tool for training throws. Remember the warm-up drill from before, where one person has to maintain their hold on the stick? We use the same start point, but this time the aim of the stick holder is to throw the person holding the stick. The aim of the person being thrown is to learn how to fall safely - so again, a two way drill. The stick is useful here as it magnifies

movement (the Wheel principle), gives us a lot more leverage and helps develop footwork. Here's a couple of simple ideas to start with.

A holds the stick with two hands, B with one. A moves the stick up and back, so throwing B backwards. From a similar set up, A steps forward, bring the stick up and out in an arc - the whipping or "fishing cast" moment we worked before against the arm. The move is powered by the stepping and wait turn, feel how you can project this movement out along the stick.

A leads B in one direction, then quickly brings the stick back another way. Again, the important thing is to project. Experiment also with level change as you move the stick. You should start with quite simple movements. As you progress, and if you partner is comfortable with it, add more twists and changes of direction into the stick movement. This creates greater challenges for the stick holder and is a god way to learn about "3-D movement."

Our next method is pretty much the same as with take downs. We begin with static positions, then we have our partner come walking in. Following that, our partner can feed in some kind of attack, be it punch, grab or kick. Escape the attack but do so in such a way that puts you in good position for your throw. For example, move with and inside a hook punch in order to get a good position for a shoulder throw.

Once everyone is comfortable, you can begin to pick up speed. In fact, some throws are easier to pull off at speed. Start to get a feel for how you can use your partner's momentum. If you are struggling, you can try this basic walking exercise to get the idea.

A walks quickly into B. In effect, B has three options here:

1. move out of the way of A
2. stay in place and move A out of the way
3. a combination of the above

So, in the first option. A moves off the line of B's approach. This can be a large movement if A wishes to escape or create distance. If A wishes to throw, they must grab B in some way - usually a wrist or arm. A can then use the direction and momentum

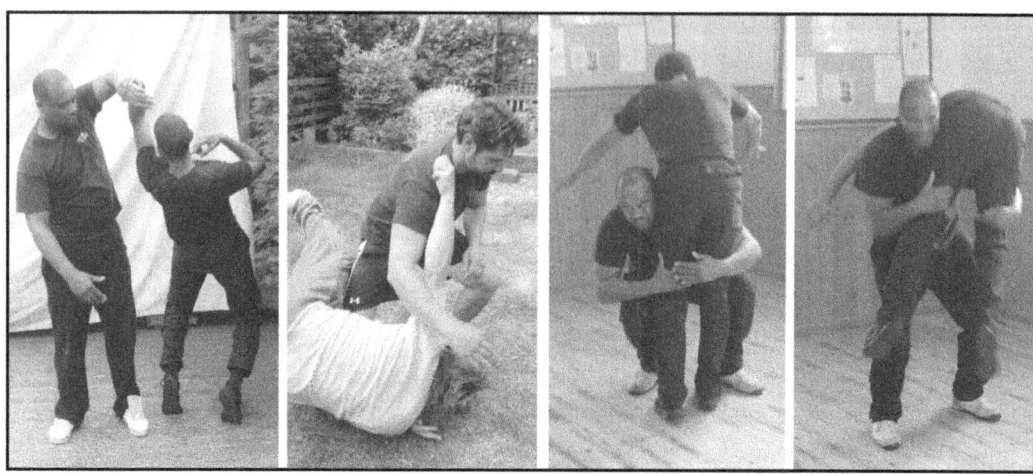

to throw B.

For the second option, A deflects B's movement - a push on B's shoulder or hip, for example. This should turn B's body and send them off to the side. Again, you can convert this into a throw or take down. Consider the level change method here too. As B gets really close, A quickly drops. This could be all the way to the floor, or A could drop to work against B's knees. From this position A may also be able to lift and throw B.

For the third option, B blends with A's movement. So as A gets close, B makes contact to slightly deflect A, but also moves with them. It might look a little like ballroom dancing, and so it should. Dancers have great blending, leading and following skills! From here, B should lightly lead A into whatever direction they wish them to go. Once you have these three ideas down, you can start working in your throws and take downs. Will you stand your ground and rotate the head? Will you move off line, grab an arm and throw? Or will you perhaps blend, rotating the body and sweeping the foot as you do so? Using this method you can gradually build up attacks and responses quite easily and safely. If you find yourself getting stuck, then hit the pause button and examine both people's body structure. The fault is usually here, or in the footwork.

Remember, for lifting throws you need to be under your partner's centre of gravity. For leverage throws, you need to pull them out of their base of support and block the hips or legs. And for all your work you should be applying power through movement and structure, not tension! Your partner should not fall at your lightest touch, nor should they put every ounce of strain in to resisting your movement. Be natural for now, this is still the learning stage.

A kneels opposite B and takes an arm. A carriers out a simple throw from this position. B has to go with the movement but turn and develop their own throw out of A's movement. All the usual principles of leverage and position apply, though it is difficult to add in any footwork here.

Once you have the idea, move to standing. Now B can add in footwork and level change / weight drop. Again, keep the throws simple at first, add in complexity as each person progresses. By complexity I mean twisting and spirals or blocking part of your partner's movement. Always take great care, applying sudden torque to a limb or joint in motion can cause damage.

## COUNTER THROWS

In much the same way we worked counter take downs, we can work counter throws. Unlike take downs we cannot wait until the throw is complete before reacting, we need to work as soon as it is applied or just as we are being thrown. This can be very challenging work and I would advise trying out only when both people are proficient and throws and falls. The best way to work into this drill is to start from a kneeling position.

Just a reminder, a great way to prepare for this kind of work is to by using a stick. Hold it in one or both hands and work your level changes. Try dropping to the floor while holding, moving around and getting back up. To increase the challenge place the stick in more uncomfortable positions. The idea is to get used to falling while the hands are holding or grabbing onto something else.

# CHAPTER SEVEN
# PINS & CARRIES

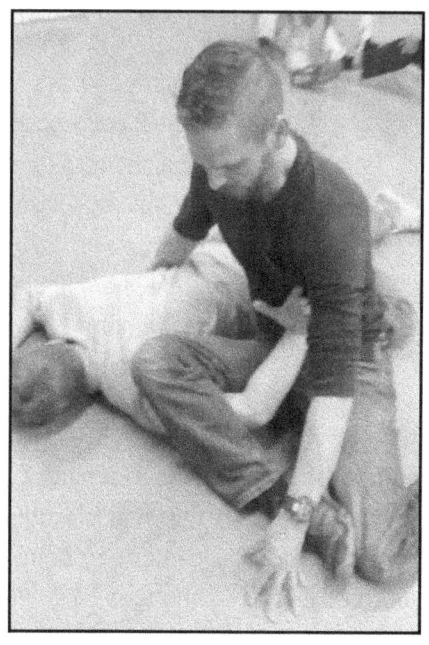

We mentioned before the two main reasons locks and hold are applied - either to pin someone in place, or to transport them somewhere else. Sometimes the pin will be followed by a further restrain - the application of cuffs, say - followed by a transport. This area also leads us into another topic, that of working as part of a team.

It can be very difficult for a single person to effectively restrain someone who is fully resistant, without resorting to strikes or similar. Of course, that is not always possible, permitted or desirable. However, two people working as a team should be able to take down and restrain almost anyone.

Here in the UK, it's not uncommon to see a group of police officers attempting to restrain a suspect, with none of their movements coordinated. Indeed, I've asked about this and found that, locally at least, police receive no training for working in pairs or more. This can result in incidents such as one guy being told repeatedly to "stop resisting" while the officers were trying to get him in the back of the van. In fact, the guy was not resisting but as one of his arms was pulled from one side, the officer on the other side interpreted that move as resistance. In effect, the officers were working against themselves.

So in this chapter we ill also talk about team work and look at some techniques for that as well as solo work. Of course, restraint work is often about more than the purely physical mechanics. How we approach, how we talk to someone, their mindset and so on are all important factors. To some extent we covered these areas in our *Systema Awareness* book but will add in a few pointers here as we go along.

## SOLO PINS

Let's assume you have taken a person down and now wish to control them on the floor. What are the principles we needs to understand? As well as the points we have already covered, there are a few more; use of weight, tension/relaxation, support, positioning, and will to resist. Let's start with a simple drill.

A is on their back. B kneels at their side. A's job is simply to sit up. B places their hands on A's body as they sit up a few times. Feel which muscles are activated / tensed in order for A to sit up.

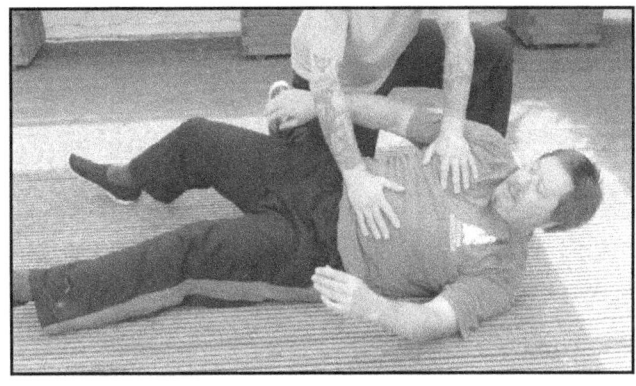

We now repeat the process. This time, as B feels the muscle begin to active, they push into it. The aim is to lock the muscle up in order to cut A's movement short. For example, if you place a hand over the stomach, you will feel it tense as A sits. Push into this tension in the right way and you will find A cannot access it. You can also link up muscles, creating a chain of tension. Try solar plexus and shoulder, for example.

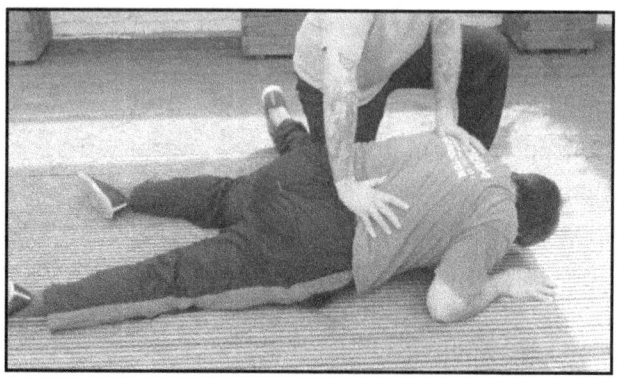

The second principle to study here is leverage. So as A is sitting, B places a hand on A's forehead and applies a little pressure, just enough to prevent the sitting up again.

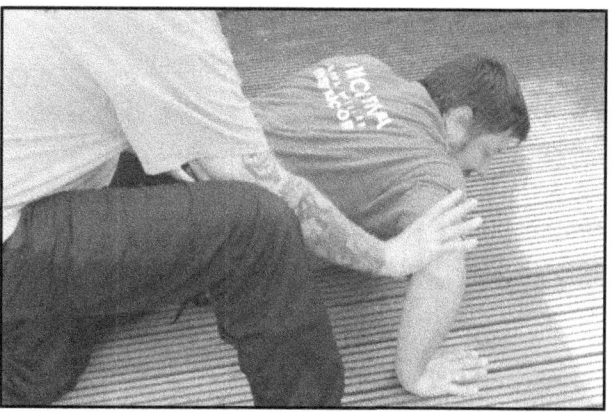

Once you have this basic idea, start working some different positions. This leads us into the principle of support. If A is on their front, they will likely place a hand under themselves and push up from it on order to raise the body. If B can take away this point of support, A cannot rise. A simple way to do this is knock the supporting arm out of line. Just rotating the elbow out will achieve this, or you can sweep the hand away from the floor.

The same principle applies with the legs. If A brings a knee up, simply knock it away again. You might also look at rotating the ankle out to the side in order to break A's structure.

We can also work the principle of weight into this drill. The most basic example of this is, as A tries to sit, B simply lays across them! Depending on the weight ratio, A should find it difficult to sit up. Try this front, back and sides again. B must learn how to fully relax in order to bring the most weight to bear on A. It can also be a good exercise for A, in learning how to roll out from under a dead weight.

The next thing for B is learning how to apply that weight through their hands, knees, or whatever part is in contact with A. When using the hands, it is tempting to lean into the movement. This will certainly bring the weight in but also compromises the structure, leaving B vulnerable to a counter. B should try and keep upright and feel how the heaviness from the body can transfer into the hands.

One way to practice this is with a standing exercise. A stands in front of B. B lifts their hands, arms very relaxed, and "drops" them onto A shoulders. Done correctly, the weight will transfer into A and buckle their knees a little. Now apply the same feeling to our ground position.

Will to resist is the next principle. This can be thought of as taking the fight out of a person. We are always trying to help people relax, to remove their aggression, to help them understand that their best course of action is to comply with your requests. Now this is a big subject in itself and, for now, we will focus on just a few basic points; pain, breathing, fear.

Pain can act to stimulate or to shut down. If you want to calm someone down, for instance, slapping them around the face is probably not going to work. A sharp, stinging slap spikes the nervous system, it usually causes a person to rear up. Of course, a very heavy slap can stun, but that's another subject. So, in our exercises above, if you want to try it, have B slap A as they try to get up. Chances are, the slap will help A, it will fire them up a bit! Instead we need the type of pain that drains a person's energy or will. Think of those times you've taken a groin shot or similar. Did you hop about shouting or did you double over and curl up moaning? So in our drill above, B now punches A in the groin, right? Well, it is an option but others are available!

From the original set up. B places hands on A. As A tries to rise now, B pushed with the hands but also jabs into A's muscles with the elbow. Short, sharp blows that help relax the muscle and give the kind of pain that makes a person pause for thought. They don't have to be super heavy blows but they should be precise in placement and in depth. The knees can also be used for this type of the work. Again, have A work from back, front and side and experiment.

Controlling a person's breathing can also help in restraint. Think about the four levels of breathing: throat, upper chest, lower chest, belly. A is on their back again and B now works to apply pressure to the above areas - one at a time or a couple together.

Feel how much pressure and which angle to apply in order to disrupt A's breathing. Simplest example. B lays with forearm across A's throat. Roll into the move a little and you will seal the airway. As before, have A move onto their side and front as well, practice the work in each position.

A word of caution here. In many places there have been a number of deaths in custody cause by something called *Positional Asphyxia*. This is where a person has had pressure applied to the torso, such as being on their front while another person has lain across their back for a period of time. Some people are very susceptible to this condition so please always exercise extreme care with any breath control work, both in training and in real life use. Where possible, I would avoid maintaining weight or pressure on the airways for anything longer than a very short space of time, and always be aware of what the person being restrained is telling you.

Controlling the breath also crosses over into our fear work. As with pain, fear can motivate or suppress. It is possible to scare someone so much, they become a better fighter. It is also possible for the toughest person to be paralysed by fear. In context of pinning a person, an appropriate approach might be to give forceful, authoritative statements as you carry out the restraint. "Hold still!" "Stay down!". That kind of thing. Keep commands short and simple. Always be positive. Never say "Don't struggle!" for example and the worst of all is shouting "Calm down!" at someone. It might help if the person understands why you are asking them to stay still, again, keep it short and simple. Speaking calmly might be a better approach in some situations, Reassure where necessary, or command when it is appropriate. Above all, stay emotionally calm and in control yourself. Anger and

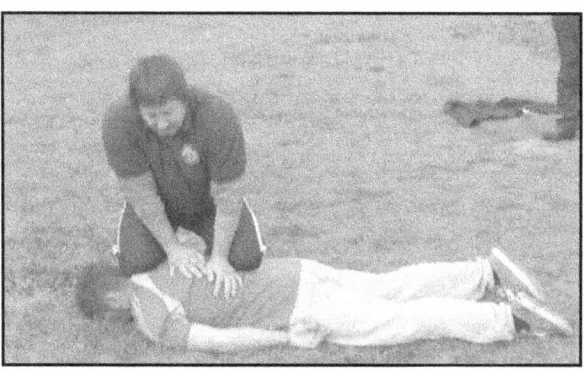

fear are highly contagious, work to relax people physically and emotionally.

So having covered some principles, let's go back to our original drill. A is on the floor, B kneeling next to them. A tries to get up and B can try all or any of the above to prevent them. Work from front, sides and back. B can also change position. Try prone, kneeling and standing. See if you can work with your feet, too. You can begin to work in different levels of speed and resistance, though remember at present you are working mostly on principles. Once you understand those, we can move on to some specific techniques. See which of the principles each of the following uses the most.

SHOULDER LOCK.

This, to me, is the best pin, assuming a relatively stable situation. By that I mean we have one person to control, we have to keep them in place while back up arrives, until they calm down, or similar. We will look at how to get into the final position first, then cover some ways to work it.

A is on their front. B kneels to the side, the right in this case. B's takes A's right hand and extends the arm out to the side. They next step over the arm with their left leg. B carefully sits as they bend the left leg, tucking A's arm in to rest on the thigh. The final position is as shown, with the left foot as close as possible to the right knee. The left knee rests on A's shoulder blade. B should maintain a straight spine. If A begins to struggle, B slightly rotates their hips forward and lifts the body a little, bringing pressure onto A's shoulder joint. A's left arm can also be lifted, or pressure on the wrist applied to increase the effect.

The advantage of this position is that B is upright and has use of both hands. One hand could be used to search A, for example. It also takes very little effort or pressure to apply this pin and once in position seems virtually inescapable. Nothing is 100% but we've not had anyone get out of this yet (and some have tried!). As always, use caution when applying, it is easy to injure the shoulder here.

So that is the finished position, how to get into it? We could work a kind of Step 1, Step 2 sequence, or "if A does that, B does that," which is okay but can never cover every situation. Instead, let's look at the factors that make this position work and how we can work into them.

The first thing is that A has to be on their front. This can be easy from a sitting position. For example, A is seated and B lunges in to grab or punch. A leans back to evade, while grabbing the attacking arm. A then pivots, swinging the legs round and into position.

Some take downs, such as the arm bar drag, put the person exactly into the right spot. Once you have the person on their front with an arm raised, just step over the shoulder with the appropriate foot and drop into the sitting position (slowly if you don't want to damage the shoulder).

Two ways then, to get into this lock I would say the only downside is that it can sometimes be a little tricky to work into the

position, but once on it is very strong. A variation is to take up a similar position against the leg. In the case A is face down again - actually it is always best to work a pin with the person face down, it is generally psychologically and physically more difficult for them to resist. This time, B has their leg crossed over the rear of A's knee,

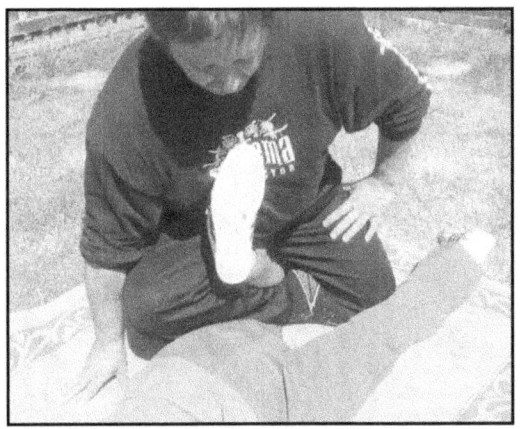
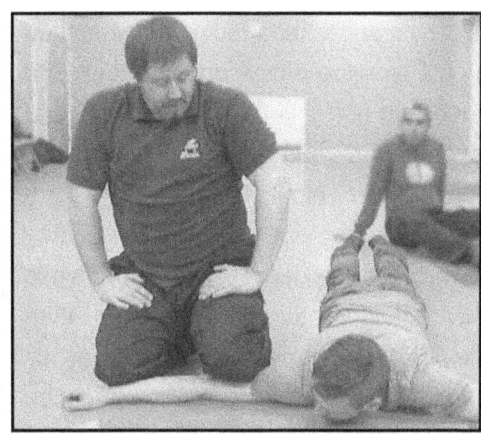

with A's shin upright, pinned against the body. All B has to do here is lean forward to apply pressure to A's knee. An ankle twist can easily be added in if required. This move might work from a floor foot takedown, given that the legs are more accessible than the shoulder.

A simpler pin is the triceps kneel. A is face down again. This time, B simply kneels on the outstretched arm. One or two knees will work and you should imagine your knee / shine bone cutting into A's muscle. A small rotation forward will help. Again, B has the advantage of being upright with hands free. Not quite as much pressure is applied to A here, though there is an element of pain compliance and B always had hands free to respond, go into a choke position, etc.

In all the above positions, one person is flat on the ground. But what if the person is on their back? On the plus side, this means we have full access to their breathing, via throat, chest and solar plexus. On the minus side, the person has full use of their limbs to try and escape or to hit and grab us. To get the person over onto their front we can try a couple of things. One is to simply grab a wrist and step over the person, using the whole arm as a lever to flip them.

Another option is to take the wrist again and pull the arm out to the side. You should be

at the person's head facing towards their feet. Place the elbow against your lead knee and use this as a fulcrum point to lever the arm round. The body will follow, coming over onto its front.

If we can't flip a person and are unable to work straight into their breathing, then we need to control as many limbs as we can as quickly as we can. We should be able to control the two nearest to us with our knees and / or a hand. It is best to keep at least one hand free. We should also be careful not to get dragged down to the ground ourselves and involved in a wrestling match, unless we are very good grapplers and it is safe to do so.

Have A taken to the floor by B, onto their back. From there, A tries to grab, hit or kick B. This leads us to another important Systema principle, *acceptance*. In this situation, this means that rather than try and block the attack from A, Be accept it and actively uses it. So for a punch, B should re-direct the punching arm and take

it across A's body. If they place A's hands on top of each other, B can now control both arms with a single hand or knee. The same principle applies with a kick. Take the attacking limb, cross it over and place it on the other leg. B should also try and use knees and elbows to pin where possible, this leaves the hands free. B should also work to keep as upright as possible, in order to avoid being pulled down and also to maintain awareness of other possible threats. Also see how you can control an arm by tucking it under your own arm. This gives you good control but again, you have your hands free.

When using any pin, particularly with the knees, always be aware of safety issues and be sensitive to the experience of the person you are pinning. If they are having real difficulties breathing or are panicking you must shift your position in order to protect their health.

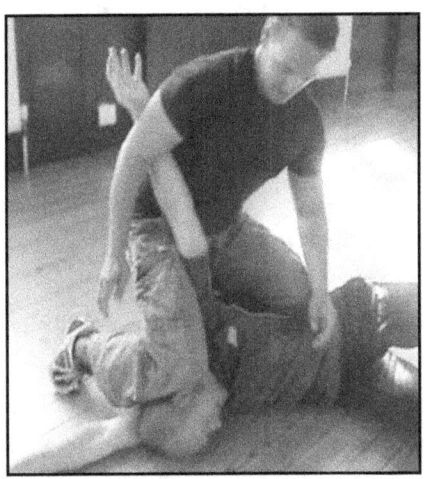

The basic finish position for this is follows. A is on their back, B has stretched their right arm out and across the upper thigh. B crosses their feet to lock in place, then simply pulls down with the hands and raises the hips to apply the lock. It is possible to escape this lock at various stages, something we will be covering in a future volume on ground fighting.

You might note here that I have not yet mentioned the classic arm bar technique. While this is a good technique to learn, I have found it is of limited value as a pin in many situations. This is because it very much ties up the restrainer. They are using both arms and both legs to restrain the other person, leaving themselves in a very vulnerable position. This may be fine in some circumstances, which is one reason for learning the technique, the other is so that we can learn to counter it.

There may be a situation where a person is so agitated or resistant the the only option is to pin them totally with your body. Of course, this again leaves you vulnerable to other threats but in some circumstance may be an option. The key here is to relax your full body weight into the person, make yourself as heavy as possible. Control the hands as much as you can but work to relax the person - verbally and through your own physical relaxation. I had a friend who worked in a secure mental unit who used this method quite often.

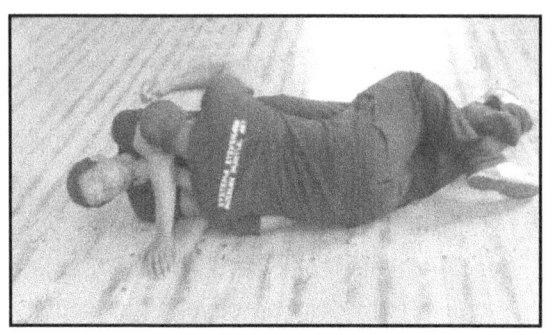

We can also use pain compliance to pin a person as well, particularly if resistance is not especially spirited. The simple wrist lock is one method. B places A's elbow on the floor, lifts the hand and applies the gooseneck lock to the wrist. If A struggles at all, B applies more pressure down into the wrist. In effect, the only escape from the pain is to remain still. You can also experiment with the nerve and vulnerable points we will be covering a little later on.

How about if a person is standing, can we pin them in place? It is more challenging, of course, though there are some options. One method is as follows. A has B place hands behind their head - a not uncommon position for an arresting officer, for example. If A thinks B may still struggle or resist from the point, they slide a thumb under B's middle finger, curls their own fingers in a little and lightly squeezes B's hand. This should lock B's hands into place. From here, A can spread B's feet and apply some pressure to to make B bend forward against the wall. While not a total pin, it is now difficult for B to do anything substantial.

If possible, the best thing to do is to use a wall as the floor - a corner works best as it restricts movement even more. But even with a single wall, if you can get the person facing it, with their toes touching the wall, they are in a weak position. Have A in that position. From here, B brings A's hand down across their back, then slides their own arm through to apply a goose neck lock. B tucks A's elbow into the body, and can also pin A's the leg with their own.

**SOLO TRANSPORTS**

Moving another person on your own can be a challenge, particularly if the person doesn't want to go. There are two options, short of incapacitating the person or verbally persuading them. We either have to make the person want to move in the

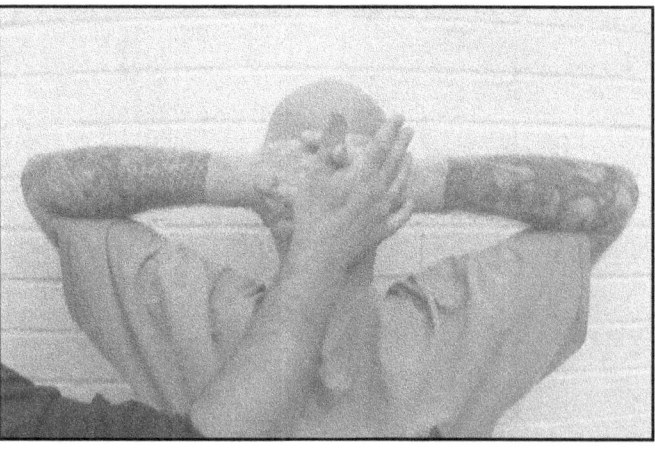

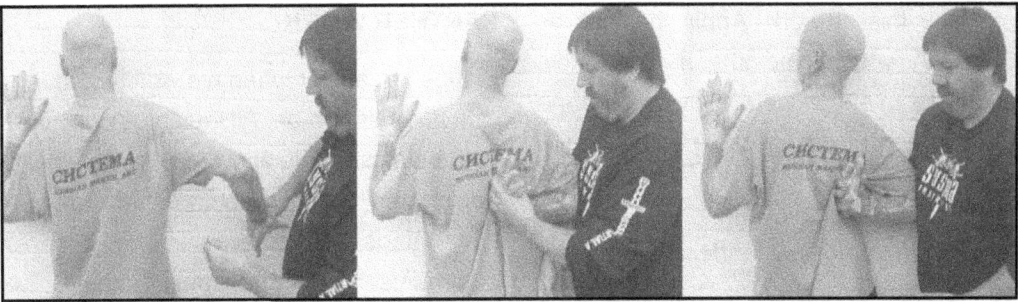

direction we take them, or control their body to such an extent that they have no choice.

Let's explore the latter first. One of the best methods I found to achieve this was what we called the Choke Carry. To practice the set up, A stands in front of B. The first task is to turn B slightly, so A gives a short, sharp push to B's left shoulder, and a pull to their right shoulder. This should turn B a little to their left. A immediately steps in and curves their right arm across B's neck, pushing back and down a little. B's right hand either grabs their own collar or, for a stronger hold, places their right palm on the side of their head.

The aim from here is to bend A back and off balance a little, forcing them to follow the movement of the head. B now moves smartly to wherever they need to go, if A struggles, B can tighten the choke hold. The key to this technique is being swift and precise in the movements, giving the person no chance to respond. You will also notice the component of balance in this drill. Think back to that idea of moving a heavy wardrobe, we tilt it. So tilting a person will always make them easier to move.

An effective way to lift a person's centre of balance is through pain compliance. If we go back to the earlier Goose Neck hold, we

can see this at work. Apply the lock as before. As you feel the other person flinch, lift a little. In effect, we are giving only one direction to move to escape the pain - upwards.

Another method is to affect a person's centre of balance directly. The pelvis is the heaviest bone in the body and, rather like the head, where it goes everything else tends to follow. This was always useful for removing people from places. A stands close to or grabs B. B pushes into the pelvis - either from the side at the hipbone, or from the rear at the small of the back. You will get the feel of the right spot with practice. B pushes forward and lifts a little. A should rise up a bit and have no choice but to follow B's direction of travel. You do need to keep the pressure on, fast and direct. Any pause and A can turn out of the movement. For this reason this method is best used to get people over short distances.

## PARTNER WORK

Things get easier when we work in tandem with another person. All the same principles of unbalancing, etc apply but we are able to apply them more efficiently. There are two key things to consider. The first is communication. The pair should be constantly monitoring or communicating with each other, verbally and through touch. A skilled pair will be able to feel their partner's movement through the person in the middle and adjust accordingly.

The second is to have a plan. If both people rush in they stand a chance of just working against each other, as already mentioned. The basic plan is to work opposites. So one goes high, one goes low, or one goes left one goes right. Let's look at a couple of methods, and also say hello to Partner C!

B and C approach A, angling in from each side. They have already planned for one to go for the left arm, one for the right. B and C each grab an arm and apply a suitable lock. In this case, A is being bent forward, allowing C to also apply head control. For the high-low option, from the same set up B will grab A's head / neck while C goes for the upper legs or a trip/sweep. This should easily take A to the ground.

A word on how B and C approach A is important here, too. As mentioned before, the verbal component is a major part of restraint work. In any situation, one partner

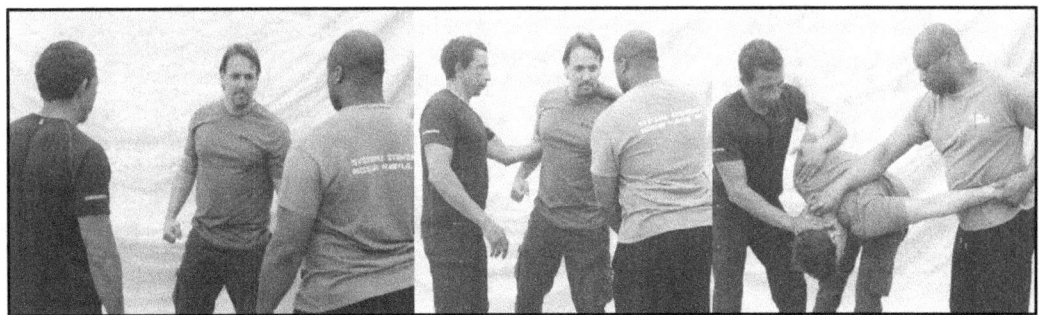

can be allocated as "the talker." The aim for this person is to keep A's attention and focus, allowing the other partner to move in close. Asking a question is always a good strategy, as it automatically engages the brain (assuming the person is lucid, that is!). It doesn't have to be talking, a loud clap of the hands or an obvious movement will draw A's gaze in the desired direction.

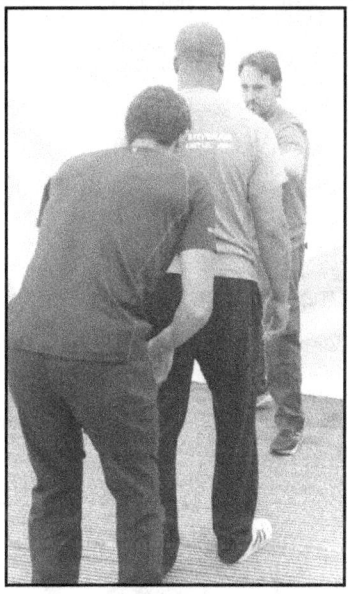

Another approach method is known as The Chain. This is where B conceals themselves behind C, who leads the approach to A, again engaging in dialogue. Once in range, B can pop out to grab whichever part of A had been agreed on.

There is also the option of having C come in from the side or rear. In this case, B is the talker. They approach A while speaking, they don't have to get too close, but do need to keep A's attention on them. C will come in from the side or rear to execute any kind of suitable take down. It might be head control, it might be a knee strike to the thigh. As soon as A's structure is broken, B comes in to assist.

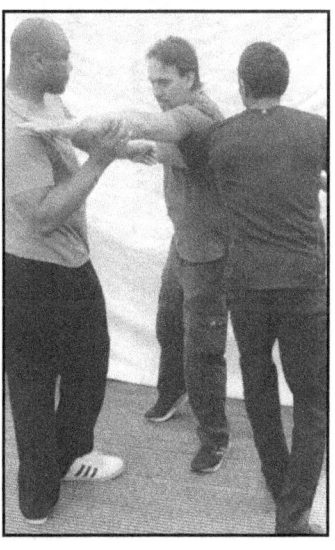

Our final variation on this works as follows. Take more care with this, as when done fast it will take A off of the ground. The set up and approach is the same, except that this time B and C grab the wrist with their outside hand. The inside hand is used to grab A's trousers just above the knee. B and C now pull A's arms out to the side as they pull A's legs from out under them. Again, watch for

A's head impacting the ground.

A nice pin from here works like this. B and C quickly tuck A's hands under their own knees. B or C now moves in to straddle A's knees with their own, effectively trapping A's hands in place.

These are very simple methods - and that is all they need to be. The more elaborate the plan, the more variables are added in, or decisions have to be made on the fly, the more prospect there is of something

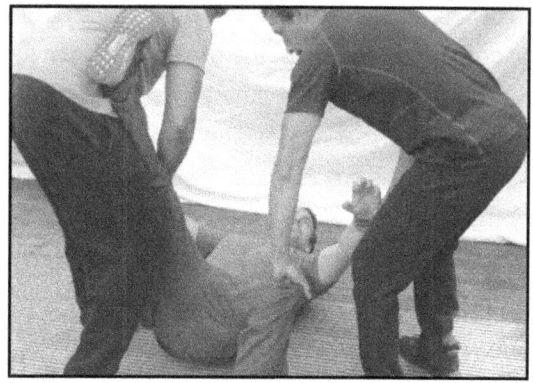

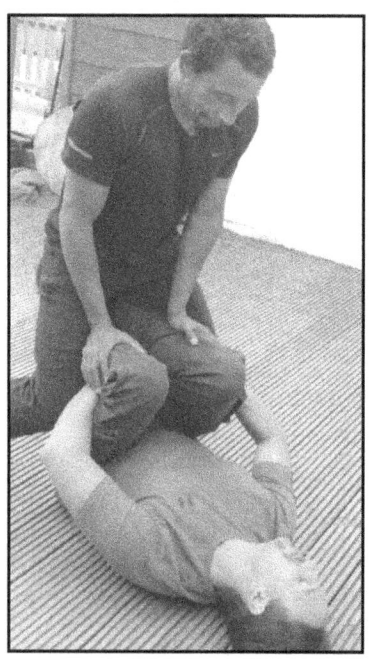

going wrong. All movements should be executed cleanly and precisely, they should be effective in the majority of "regular" situations.

But having controlled a person, how do we pin them? Again, we give each partner a defined role. For pinning, we can stick for sides or high-low. B can sit on A's legs while B controls the upper body, for example. Or we might have one partner pin while the other stands over them - this allows for the use of arm bars and other techniques that tie up the restrainer. Any of the methods already described can be used, solely or in combination.

How does a pair then work to transport someone? Let's start with two basic ideas, both from a standing position. For these, B and C are working the left-right method. A stands, B and C each take one of A's wrists. They now lift and twist, in what is sometimes called the Chicken Wing position. This lifts A's centre of gravity and allows B and C to walk A way.

The second version is known as the Prisoner Carry. Here, B and C approach from behind and grab A's wrists again, with their outside hands. Now, B and C bring their other hands across A's chest and grasp hands. To move A, B and C now pull down a little on A's hands and lift their nearest shoulder / chest. The aim is to lock A's arms a little and also to raise them up onto tip toe. From here, the prisoner can be transported away.

## LIFTING

We have discussed pin and transport as either / or but there are occasion when we

need to do both - restrain a person in place, then, once they are no longer a threat, move them to another location. As most pins are on the floor, how do we get a prone person up to transport them? Here's a few ideas, for both solo and partner work. As mentioned before, these methods may also be useful if you have to transport an injured or perhaps inebriated person!

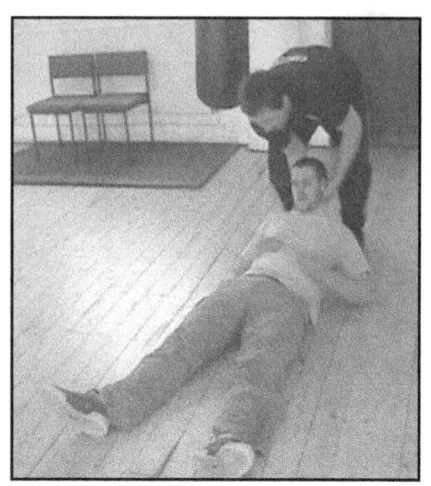
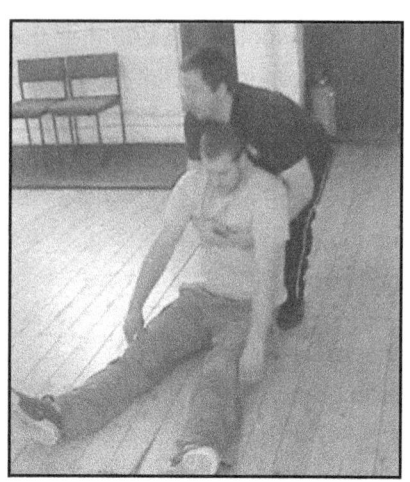

If you need to keep the lock on, then maintain pressure. This will usually be an arm lock of some type of perhaps a choke. Hard to move someone and maintain a leg lock! So let's say that A has B pinned with a wrist lock. A first needs to tell B that he needs them to stand, as they will be moving away. If B complies, then no problem, though of course A should always remain alert and in control of the situation. If B is less keen to stand, A needs to provide some motivation. This may be achieved verbally, or through the use of our principles already discussed. If A bends B's arm, the wrist lock now becomes a lifting motion rather than a pinning motion. The pain will hopefully cause B to stand. The lock can then be converted into a carry type, as before.

So some pins can be translated into "lifts", through pain compliance. Another "pain lift" is for A to kneel at B's head, place the thumbs just behind the ears and push in and up. You might need to feel around to find the exact point and angle. When it goes in, B will sit up. From that position A can work under the arms to lift B. Now, with this being a nerve point method it won't work on everyone, so bear that in mind.

LEOs will cuff a person when down. This makes things easier as you can use the cuffs to lift the person. In other settings, you may be able to improvise with belts, laces, etc, which we will cover in a later chapter. Clothing is another possible handle. You

might be able to lift someone up by the scruff of their jacket - though watch they don't wriggle out!

If the person is non-resistant or injured / unconscious then we have to consider two things when lifting them. Will our lifting cause further injury and also we must ensure we do not injure ourselves. A good method is to use the previous pressure point sequence, without pushing on the nerve points. Get the person sitting, then squat, place forearms under the arms and lift, keeping the back straight.

We mentioned the fireman's lift and carry before, this is a good method to practice from both a practical and a fitness point of view! The carrier should be very sure to maintain good posture and keep their steps quite short, especially if jogging.

There is another solo lifting method that got a lot of attention on social media a while back. It has become known as the Ranger Roll, though I'm not sure of its exact origins. In effect, the lifter rolls across the other person, grabbing an ram as they go. I suggest you seek it out on Youtube or similar to see it in action, that will give you a much better idea of how it works.

If lifting in pairs, one good carry method is the Chair. Here, the pair either hold a leg each or link arms underneath . The other arms link to give support at the back. This is probably the most comfortable carry.

# CHAPTER EIGHT
# EQUIPMENT

Working empty hand in a dangerous situation is not an ideal position to be in. Even a "low level" confrontation can escalate quickly, so it is good to be aware of items we can use to help protect ourselves. Of course, there are more specialist items, such as handcuffs, batons and so on that may be used in a professional environment. But outside of that it is useful to know how to use any everyday items that might be around, as well as clothing - our own and others.

When it comes to weapons or equipment, we should be very wary about placing too much stock in what is, in effect, an inert object. Picking up a stick, for example, can give us a feeling of confidence or power, a feeling that may be misplaced. Any weapon is only a tool and should not be fetishised or invested with more power than it has. Personally I'm not a fan or "tacticool" pens or similar, I feel you can achieve the same with everyday items.

Another thing to consider is that rather than learn how to use every single item specifically, our approach is to learn how to apply our general Systema principles to the item and circumstances at hand. Having said that, there are specific ways to use different types of item. To keep things straightforward, we shall divide our work into flexible and fixed.

**FIXED**

This covers anything solid, such as a pen or similar, a baton, short stick, broomstick, a chair, a firearm, even a tree or post! As there is no give, these items are primarily used to assist in locking joints, or to assist in pain compliance. Of course, they can be used to strike as well, and may be particularly useful in "relaxing" muscles but we will put that work to one side for the moment.

To illustrate our first drill progression, we will start with a stick. In fact, we will revisit the earlier drill, where one person held the end of a long stick and follows its movement. We begin with the same set up - A holds the stick out, B grips the end. The aim now is for A to see how they can lock up B's wrist, elbow and / or shoulder. Start with very basic movements. For example, A circles the stick in and round and rests the stick end across B's wrist. We now have a similar position to the arm bar from earlier. A can then push forward and down to lock and take down.

If B has grabbed the stick a little higher up, or if it can be slid, A can push the end under B's armpit, to lock the whole arm. This teaches us how to understand and utilise tension in our partner. In this case, once A pushes into the tension, they may be able to put B in such a position that they cannot move the arm or hand. The tension created in the forearm should be such that they are unable to even let go of the stick, or move out of the position. In effect, they lock themselves through their own tension. When done correctly you can pin a person to the floor with this method, or leave them in place to figure out how to try and escape!

Another option is for A to take the other end of the stick under B's arm and over the shoulder, in order to set up a shoulder lock. A can also take the stick all the way across to set up a choke position.

If A grab's the stick with both hands. B can use a similar movement in order to cross A's arms. This position can be used to either break the grip or to lock A's arms in place.

Every now and then have B change the position of the grip. They can hold with a single hand at one end, in the middle, use two hands to grip and so on. Each change offers new possibilities to locking. Against two hands, A might circle one end of the stick through and over the inside of B's arm, then push the end down to the floor. This should distort B's structure and, due to their own tension, "stick" them in place.

We can also use the stick to initiate locks. A approaches B and places the stick under B's right arm. A grabs the top end of the stick and rotates it forward and down. They move to B's side as they do this, so locking the arm with the stick. Depending on the angle of approach and how the stick is pace, it is also possible to leave one end of the stick in place.

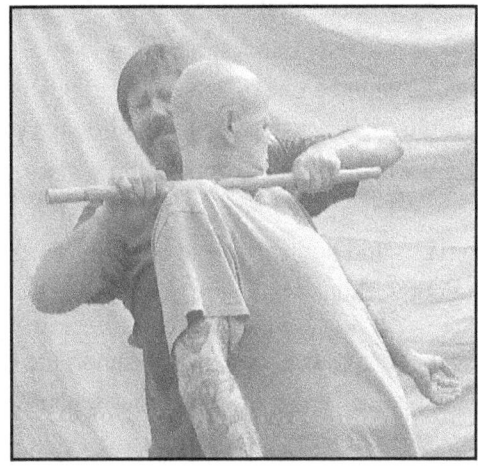

The stick can be used to reinforce most locks, in particular chokes. For safety, work into the side of the neck rather than across the windpipe. This is a very good method to use as a transport as it gives the stick holder a lot of control. Do not just pull back with the stick but rotate it forward as you press down and back. This should have the effect of also breaking the structure, making the upper body lean back. Think back to our earlier triangle point work.

The stick can also be used to help us escape from grabs and holds. We start with the wrist again. A holds the stick and B grabs their wrist. First A should see how much mobility they have in the wrist and how

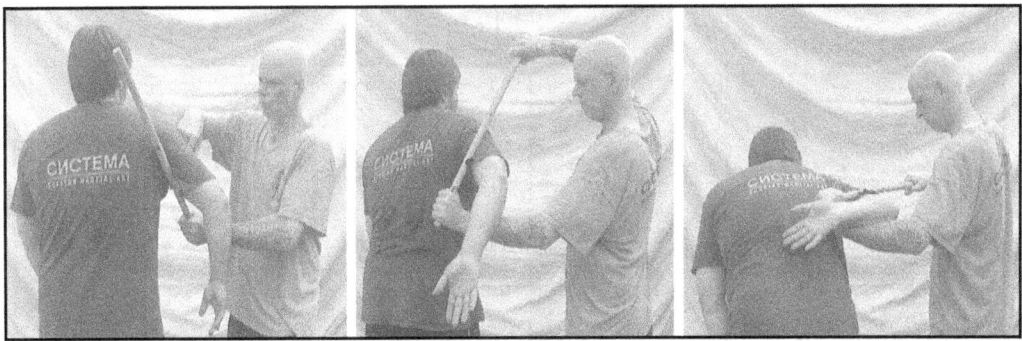

many different angles they can move the stick too. A simple escape method from a single or double grab is for A to bring the butt end of the stick up, turn the wrist inward, then press down with it. A may be able to trap / hook B's other hand with the bottom of the stick, or can continue the circle round to lock the opposite elbow. Again, experiment with the numerous variations you can work from this start position.

You may notice that for this type of work the stick is primarily used against the joints. The key, as with the choke, is not just to push but to rotate the stick into the joint. Adding a turn of the waist and/ or dropping the weight will also assist in the escape. So next have A come in and apply grabs to different parts of the body. B uses the stick to escape.

Against a choke, B could work either into the wrist or the inside of the elbow. This is all assuming that for some reason B simply doesn't want to or can't just hit A with the stick! Remember to apply that rotation again.

Against a double grab, the stick can go under one arm and over the other. A simple twist of the waist should then break the grip. Push one end of the stick up and pull the other down.

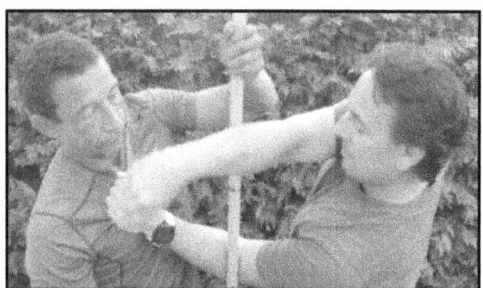

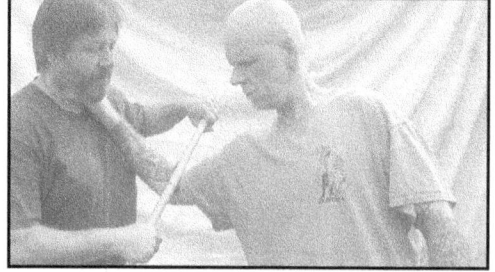

A long stick can be used against the legs. A grabs B who places the end of the stick onto the floor behind A's nearest leg. B pushes down on the stick then rotates it into the rear of A's knee. Again, the rotation is key here to collapsing the structure.

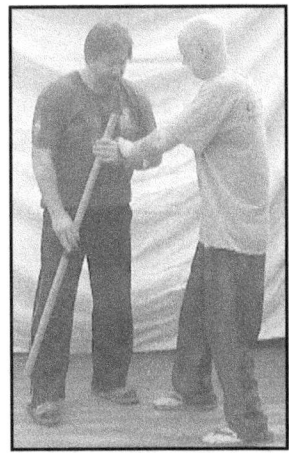 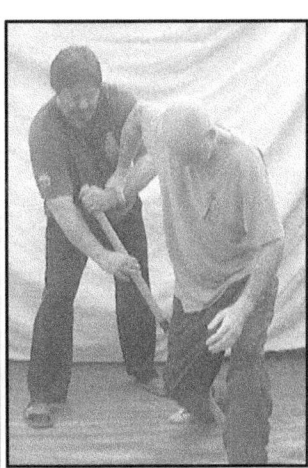

The long stick can also be used against the legs as a take down. To practice, have a stand in position. B places the end of the stick between the feet. They then rotate the stick out, across the inside of the nearest knee. As this leg moves out, B immediately takes the stick back across the inside of the other leg. The end of the stick should remain quite firmly on the ground and the movement again relies on rotation rather than just pushing.

 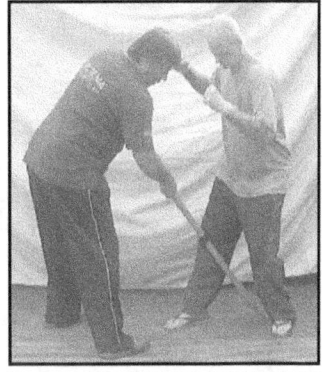

The second move can also be carried out as more of a strike. Once you have the idea, try working it from some different angles and start points.

The next step is to work with different lengths of "stick", from a pen through to a long stick (for pen here I mean anything roughly that size and shape.) The first step is to get used to handling the time. If you can't handle something with ease normally, you will never manage it under pressure. So get used to moving the item around in your fingers, try working with different grips and so on.

The good thing with smaller items is that they are easily concealed and, also, do not look like weapons. On the other hand they are not able to inflict any major damage on an

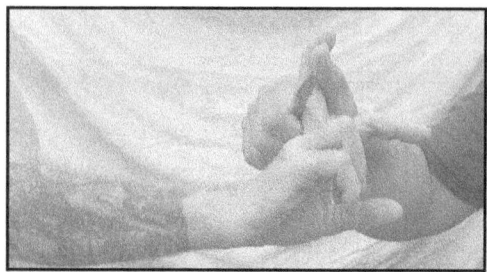

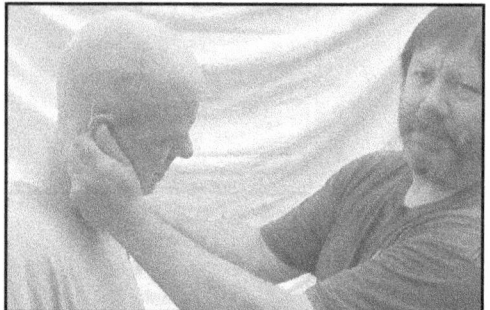

attacker, apart from in one or two obvious places. These items, then, are generally used to reinforce a movement or technique. Take small joint locks, for example. We can use the pen to reinforce a finger lock.

We can also use the item to reinforce other types of grab, to soft tissue areas such as the ear or the cheek. In this case, we roll the pen in with the fingers. If guiding a person from this type of position remember to add in your waist movement or wave movement rather than just pulling from the hand.

A pen or stick can also be used to work into nerve points or vulnerable areas. This may be to reinforce a movement, to improve pain compliance or to create tension in a person.

Once you have some ideas with a pen, look around at other objects that will give a similar effect. The corner of a book, for example, the edge of a metal ruler, keys, maybe even a rolled up magazine. Anything that has a reasonably solid edge or end can be used.

Another useful item for restraint is a chair. The first thing, as with any new object, is to get used to handling it. Chairs come in all shapes and sizes In the photos, for example, we are using a plastic garden chair. On the positive side this is light and easy to move. On the negative side, the legs are quite short and its lack of weight means it may buckle or not be as effective for some techniques. A chair with longer metal legs may be easier to apply locks with, it may also be heavier and less easy to wield.

So get used to working with different types of chair. Spend a moment to lift them, move them around, rotate them. Then you can being with some simple techniques. In effect, a chair gives us four stick to work with, so much of the locking work will be the same.

A grabs a leg of the chair. B experiments with rotating the chair around in order to lock the wrist, as with the earlier stick movement.

From the same start point, B next explores how they can use two legs of the chair. A simple turn will bring one leg to the elbow while the other locks the wrist.

If A grabs the chair itself, B simply rotates one leg over A's elbow and pushes forward and down slightly. If B turns to the side A will be taken to the floor.

The chair can also be used against the legs. The leverage created by rotation of the chair can be very powerful. It works best when applied to the right points on other other person's structure. Behind the knee is a good spot, especially if another leg is laced across the front of the thigh. From that position it takes just a slight turn of the chair to buckle a person's base. The twisting movement can be a turn or lean of the body but you should also experiment with wave movement too. When you work, try and keep the pressure even and your movements smooth. This will give the other person less chance to work back against the chair. Should they grab it, you can work into one of the arm lock type movements from above.

Another way to use a chair is to help us control or pin a person, whether to the floor to a wall. This is where a heavier chair works best.

Start by placing the chair legs around your partner and twisting the chair. See how much pressure you need to distort their structure. Again, placing the chair legs on the right spots will help. Next repeat the same work with your partner on the floor, then finally against a wall.

There is a very important thing to remember when using the chair - or any other object, for that matter. It is that you can let go of the object! Don't get locked onto it yourself. If your opponent grabs the chair, maybe let them have it - drop it and immediately do

something else while their hands are occupied. Once you have a feel for the chair you can begin to work this into your drills. Your partner may respond by grabbing the chair, trying to escape from it, hitting you and so on.

One last use for the chair for now and that is as a barrier . A rushes into B, who pushes the chair into them as they get close. This should make A stumble and give B a chance to grab and gain control for a take down or similar.

Of course, there are many other items that can be used in a similar way to sticks and chairs. While each has its own characteristics we should not feel we have to learn separate techniques for each one. Instead, assess each object and how it can be used. A military shovel, for example, has a stick element but the spade part can be used to hook into joints.

We might also consider professional work with weapons, and with weapon retention in

particular. It may be there are situations where use of force is limited, in which case studying use of the weapon for restraint purposes is useful. Again, much of this will relate back to the regular stick work, along with the extra opportunities for hooking, depending on the type of weapon in use.

## FLEXIBLE

This covers items such as clothing, belts, rope, handcuffs, and so on. Clothing is mostly used as a handle, though it can also be used to choke. Belts and rope cuffs have obvious uses in tying a person up, which can run all the way through to specialised tying methods (particularly in the Japanese arts.) Likewise, cuffing a suspect is primarily a function of LEOs and is usually trained with procedural considerations in mind.

Let's start with a basic method for clothing. For this type of work it's best for people to wear old jackets, jumpers etc that they

don't mind getting stretched or ripped. It is also good to work with clothing that is time and place appropriate. For example, if you live in the tropics how many people will you encounter wearing a heavy winter coat?

We should also bear in mind that clothing being used is a two way street. If you are wearing a hood, you are as vulnerable to having it pulled over your face as the other person is. For this reason we should also include the use of clothing in our escape drills.

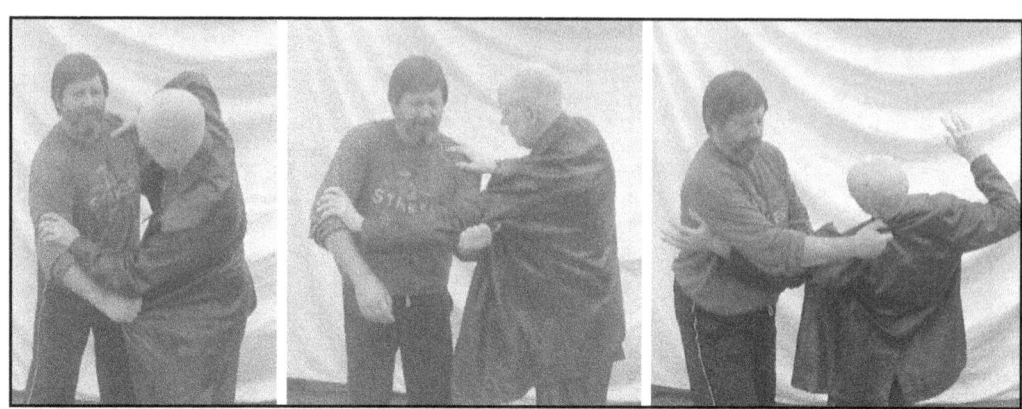

To start, A stands opposite the suitably clothed B and starts to pull and manipulate the clothing to break B's balance. It is easy to do this by pulling back on a hood, for example. Tugging sharply downward on a sleeve should bring the wearer down. Look at how pockets can be used to grab and pull, they make good handles (if the stitching is up to par!). Even just grabbing lapels can give you a strong handle on a person - but be aware of how you grab! The best way to grab is to slide your fingers down the material, then curl them in, as though you are making a fist.

Repeat, but this time B and grabs the jacket or coat and sees how they can move A around I not by pulling with the arms, but by working with the shoulders and hips. Think of the wave movement, you are putting this through the other person. Don't just think about using the hands, either. If a person has a longer coat on, pull the bottom part out, then use your knee to pull and bring the person down.

Run this as a static drill first, then have B come in and apply a simple grab. A responds by using B's clothing in some way to unbalance / take down. As before, vary speed and other factors as required.

Clothing can also be used to restrain. A very "old school" method, from back in the day when chaps always wore jackets, was to pull the jacket out and down, so pinning the bounder's arms before administering a sound thrashing! Pulling the clothing over a person's head/face will disorientate them, particularly if you combine it with breaking

 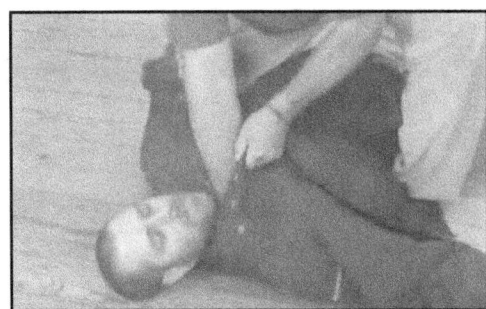

the structure This is very useful for transport work.

Clothing can also be used for chokes. Jackets work best but it is possible to even use t-shirts. One method is to grab the lapels. Pull one hand down while the other

further pin a person or to choke them out. This time, one hand uses a reverse grip and pulls the collar across the neck towards the opposite shoulder. The other hand grabs the lapel and pulls it upward and back towards the choker.

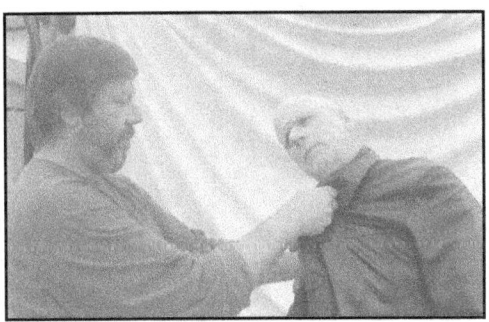 

pulls the material across the throat. This can either be a choke or a sudden movement to pull B off balance. This type of choke also works well on the ground, to

Sometimes the clothing can be used to reinforce the choke. Here, the collar is grabbed by the choking hand and pulled in to make the choke tighter. The other hand

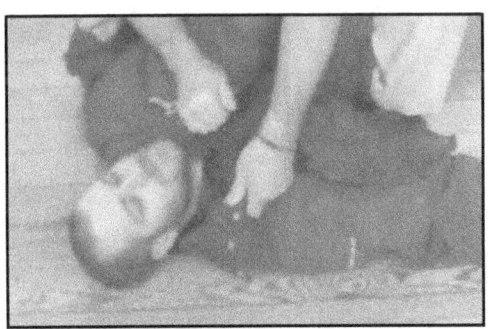 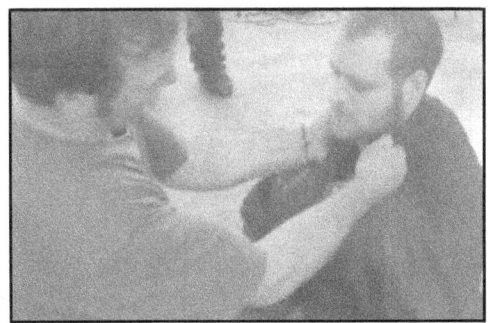

and twist it up around the neck. In this way you use the shirt as you might a scarf or rope.

We can also use clothing to help pin and control, though with the caveat that it can also tie up our own hands. So grabbing a collar and pushing a person into a wall may pin them but it also leaves their hands free to work back against us. In general, if using a wall we are better pinning the person face first into it. This makes it more difficult for them to use their hands and if we grab the scruff of a a coat or jacket we can usually pin them with one hand

can also be used to make the hold stronger. Another option is to grip the collar then pull down while curling the knuckles inward.

Once you have the feel of chokes with a jacket, you can try the same with t-shirts and other items of clothing. Generally these will have more give in them but it is still possible to work with the collar. Work your grip into the seam as before and pull across. Another option is to place your hand inside the t-shirt

Another thing to explore is how clothing helps us carry out our normal take downs. In this

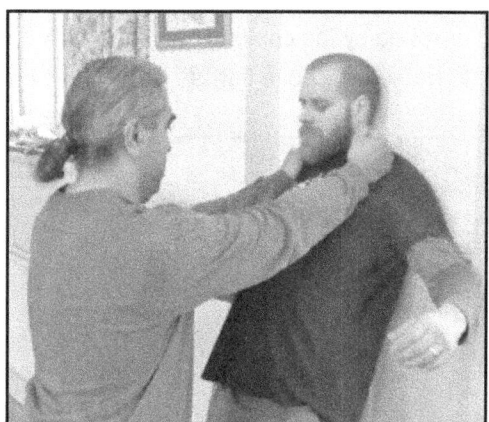

case, we pull sharply on the lapel to bring the person forward. Then place the thumb into the clavicle notch and press in and down, driving from the elbow.

The other aspect of clothing is using it to escape if we are grabbed. Think about what you are wearing. What opportunities does it offer for someone to grab and control you? Practice getting your jacket on and off quickly.

The next stage is to have your partner give you a simple grab, by the lapels, for example. See how quickly you can work out of the jacket. Staying relaxed will help. In a way you think of it as escaping a hold, all the same principles apply. Which space can you move into, where is the path of least resistance and so on.

From there, can you now use the item of clothing against the other person? If you have been quick, they will still be holding it, so their hands are occupied! Work to flow from your escape movement into a counter. Take the jacket across there throat, for example and into a takedown or choke.

Take the time to examine all your items of regular clothing and see the dangers and potential in each. A long scarf may keep you warm, it also gives an attacker a very easy handle by which to control you.

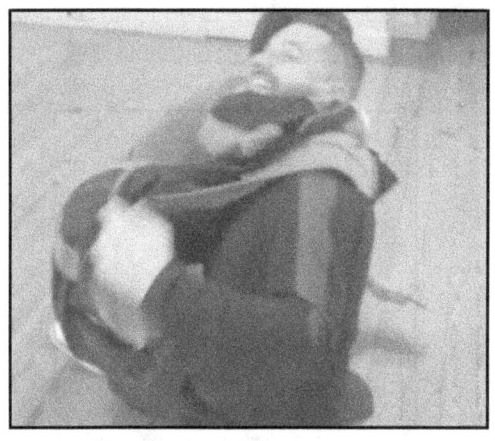

Even shoelaces can be useful! If you need to immobilise someone's hands and don't

have cuffs, once you have them face down, use a shoelace to tie their thumbs together

A belt is a common item and can be used in many ways. Like laces, a belt can be used as makeshift cuffs. The first thing we have to know is how to loop the belt correctly. Fold the belt in half to make a loop. Push the loop through the buckle. Next, pull the end of the belt out through the buckle. This then gives you a loop which you can tighten by pulling on the end of the belt.

This is easily used to tie up hands, just place the loop over the wrists and tighten. Incidentally, though we are restraining the hands in front here, for clarity, it is better to tie the hands behind a person. Hands in front, even if tied, can still be used to hit or club! Of course the restraint could also be applied

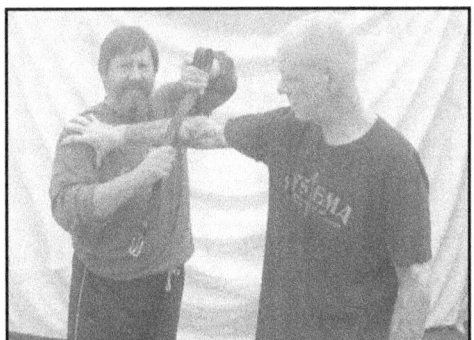

around the elbows or knees. We can also work the "normal" belt around the neck. As a choke, in which case we rotate the knuckles inward, or as a transport. A belt can also be used to reinforce take downs. From a grab, place the belt inside the elbow joint, for example, and pull down and inward.

If you are holding the belt and your wrist is grabbed, keep one hand in place. Take the other end of the belt around the neck, then pull down and to the side sharply. Reinforce the movement by also lifting the grabbed hand.

Most work with equipment comes down to experimenting with all the different items you have available. There are specialised restraint items available, of course, but I prefer to work with things that I find close to hand. Also get used to seeing your environment in a practical context, too. People can be jammed into corners, have arms twisted around tree branches, have wrists locked by a steering wheel, and so on. Be creative and practical in your outlook but remember the items are only there to reinforce our basics and their underlying principles. Don't get too psychologically or physically hooked into the item itself.

# CHAPTER NINE
# UN/FRIENDLY WORK

For this chapter we will begin to work a little deeper and also cover some other situations and scenarios we might find ourselves in. We will start with what we might call "everyday bodyguard" work.

People often think of Close Protection as a professional undertaking, which it is, of course. However, if we go out with our kids especially, we are all bodyguards. We watch our kids to make sure they are safe, steer them away from danger, and so on. The same applies to family and friends, or even in circumstances where a person may need some assistance or help. There are wider considerations in all of these cases, awareness, communication, etc but we will focus here on the purely physical aspects of friendly take downs, movement and interventions.

## ASSISTANCE

Imagine you are with a person and you need to either get them to the floor, or quickly move them out of the area. This could be for something as minor as moving them out of a busy doorway all the way up to an active shooter situation.

The first thing to note is that all our usual principles still apply. Balance doesn't change depending on the situation, it is a constant (unless you are fighting on the moon, perhaps. Let me know how that goes). This means we can use any of our previous work, just with a mindset of being careful how we bring the person to the floor.

There are two methods I find work best for this. The first uses the inside arm takedown. A takes B's wrist, pulls the arm out a little, then curves in and down on the inside of the elbow. The second uses the knee. A moves in close to B, nudges a knee forward to buckle it and slower lowers B to the floor.

The preparation for all this work lies in our earlier training - because at first, we should be lowering our partners gently to the ground rather than slamming them down, both to develop our own accuracy and sensitivity and also to protect them in the initial stages of training. Besides which, it is always useful to have a gradable response to a situation. If your default is always to grab someone's ears, sharply twist and throw them to the floor with a smack, well, that might be appropriate in some situations. In others, say you have to do it to your child, or perhaps a person with mental issues or under the influence of a substance, it may not be so appropriate, especially if you are being observed

So a useful side-effect of learning "friendly" work is that is develops adaptability in our response as well as further reinforcing our mindset of being calm and professional" rather than a "raging beast." Youtube is full of grimacing gougers, snarling ear rippers and the like, the real world is somewhat more nuanced and less like an action movie.

Take the two take downs above as a starting point and begin to find your own variations. Use of clothing is another good option, as we have already seen. For now, it is enough to understand that a mechanical take down is like any simple machine, it is multi-functional.

Another aspect of friendly work is helping someone out. If may be someone you know, it might be a complete stranger. Let's set up a situation. A has grabbed B in a bearhug. C wishes to help B. In the particular position, A is wide open for strikes, of course, but let's assume they re not appropriate. First off, C should look at the position of A's hands and the direction they are exerting force in - in this case, inwards. If C pushes A forward, they will only increase the pressure on B. So C needs to take A back, in the opposite direction. We think back to our earlier methods. Controlling the head is always a good option. So C could manipulate B's head, at the same time doing something to the legs. If A is falling back, they are unlikely to maintain the grip on B. The natural response is to bring the arms out to the side - though C should always be prepared for things to go wrong.

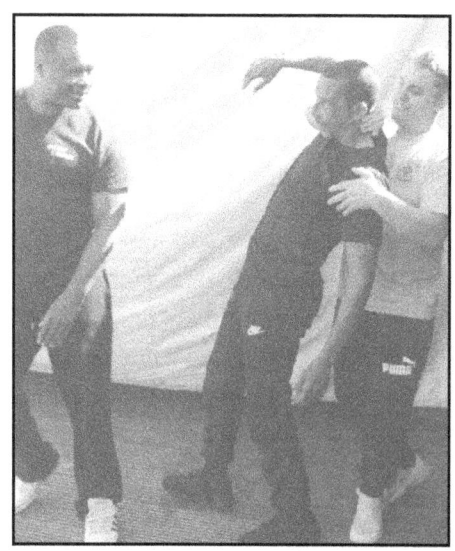

 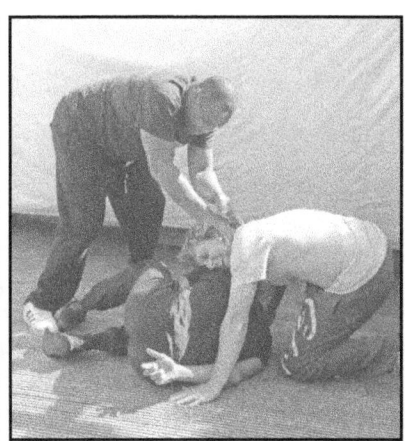

This kind of work is usually straightforward, as the target has hands occupied and is wide open for a takedown. Of course, you don't have to wait until things get that far, we can also get a person in a hold before they reach our friend. Again, if their attention is focused on someone else it makes our job that much easier.

In other situations we may have to intervene in a situation, split people up, stop them fighting and so on. Again, as their attention is on each other the work is simple enough if we observe a couple of principles. The first is the golden rule of working against more than one person - try to bring them together somehow so you can work on them as one person. Imagine getting in the middle of them, you become a target. Or try working against one while fending off the attacks of the other - difficult. Instead, try and keep them both in contact. Cross their arms over - if one has grabbed the other don't break the grip, push one into the other and so on.

The second principle is to observe where the centre of balance and mass / tension is. For example, if both are bent forward in a clinch, the weak point of balance is straight down between them. To train this have A and B wrestle. C takes a second to observe, then moves in to control both. In this case, pressing down on one person's head takes both to the floor.

Another example. A is hooked in quite deep, it may not be possible to separate A and B. Or it might be that C has to control both people, say in a doorman type situation. C needs to observe the body structure of A and B. In the example above, see how both fighters are leaning forward into each other. This tells us that the point of balance is weakest directly down and forward. C should then apply downward pressure to A and B simultaneously. It may be necessary to add in a slight rotation. This should bring both A and B down to the floor.

Sometimes you only need to work against one person, especially if they have a deep lock or hold on the other. This is an issue with deep holds - when we apply them we also lock ourselves up. In this case, A has B in a front choke. C moves in and brings A's hips back and down. This forces A to sit, also bringing B with them. The forward

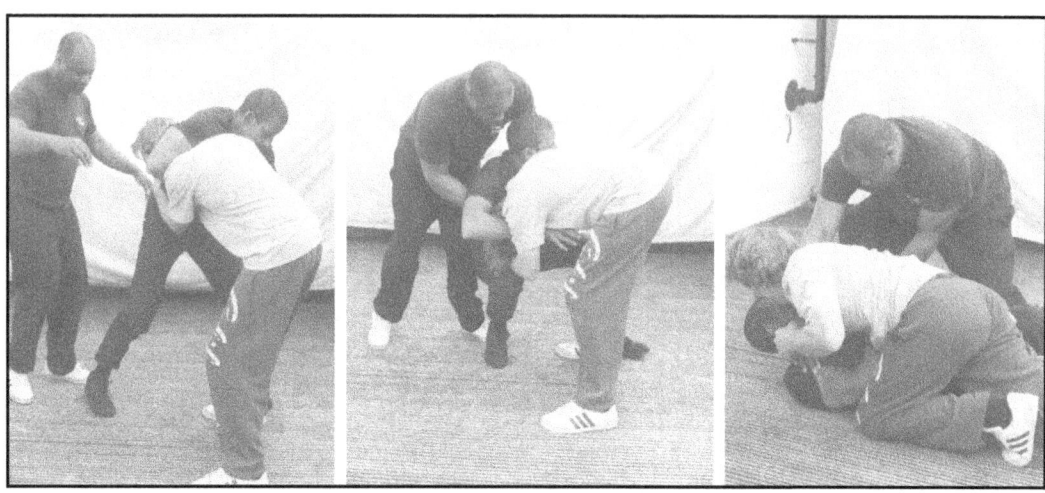

momentum and weight of B takes A to the floor, hopefully releasing the grip. In effect this is a sacrifice throw but using someone else as the sacrifice!

To practice this work, have your training partners stand in different positions, one or both applying grabs. Work first into the structure, feel for the balance points, see how you can move the feet of one or both. Once you have that, begin working takedowns. From there, work with your partners moving. They can both be struggling, or one can be an aggressor. The challenge at this stage is to work without striking, we are working purely on structure and balance.

You can also work as part of a pair of course, so now A and B, plus C and D!. The same partner principles apply as in our previous work - be prepared, have a simple plan, communicate. You may come to a point, whether solo or partner, where A has a hold or grip that is simply too strong for you to break with a take down. This leads us into working against resistance, which we will be covering shortly.

One word on taking down two or more people. Try to take them down in such a way that one lands on top of the other. If the people are attached, this should not be too difficult. From this position. All you have to do is pin the top one to pin both. Trying to

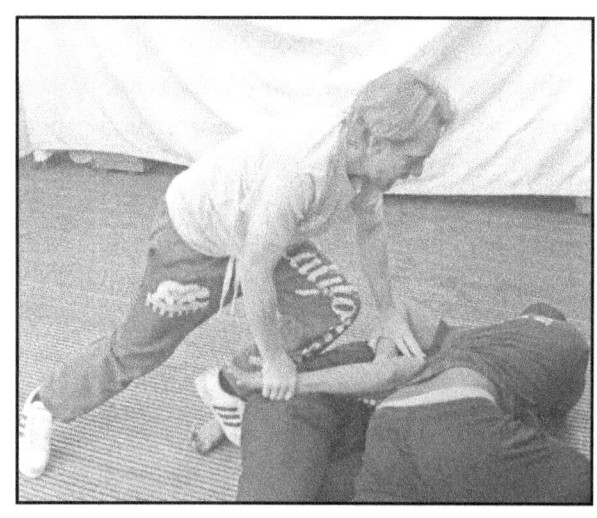

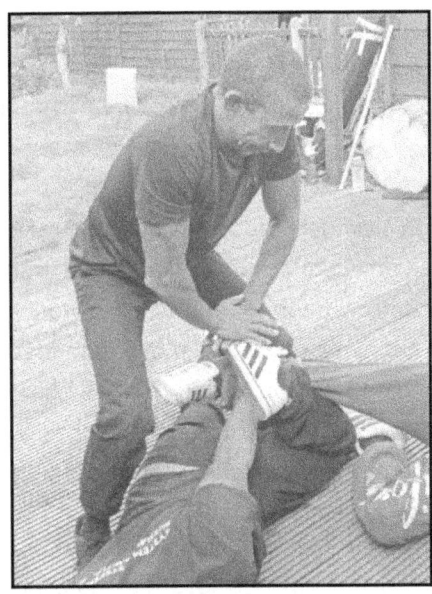

pin two separate people on the floor is virtually impossible on your own. If the pair are not close, you can use the limbs of one to pin the other. For example, pressing the feet of A into B's arms.

## JOINT BREAKS

From friendly work to distinctly unfriendly! In fact, to quote the great Basil Rathbone these are "actions inimicable to good fellowship!"

It is often said in martial arts that a joint lock is actually a break not carried out to its full extent. For most general self defence situations these should hopefully not be required. Still, it is good to study them for two reasons. One, they may be required in some circumstances. And two, they are part of the overall study of how the human body works on a mechanical level. Another thing to consider is that the perceived threat of a joint break tends to make a person relax and/or move in a particular direction. In that sense, the threat of a joint break can be used as a method of control.

The three areas most vulnerable to breaks are the fingers, elbows and knees. The methods already covered on these only needs a little more pressure added to change from lock to break, so most of the work has already been done. However, there are some extra specifics we can look at. A word of caution before we start, it can take surprisingly little force to damage an /extended joint so proceed with caution.

A simple technique is to use the shoulder against the elbow joint. A grabs B's lapel. B grips the attacking wrist, turns and drops a little and brings A's arm over their shoulder. The elbow should be resting just on the top of the shoulder here. B now has

a very strong lever position, hand pulls down, shoulder goes up, with which to attack A's elbow joint.

One method unique to Systema (in my experience) is using the body to break the arm. The set up for practice goes like this. A stands opposite B and feeds in a punch to the face. B rolls their shoulder up in order to protect the chin and deflect the punch. Get this working a few times first. Next, as B yields to the push, they swing up their right hand to trap A's wrist against the body. It doesn't have to be a grab, a simple pin will do.

B now - carefully at first - rolls their left shoulder forward. This should bring either the shoulder or the upper arm in contact with A's elbow. A should feel the pressure on the joint already. That is the position. To bring power into the movement. B applies a wave across the shoulders, from right to left. This will bring A a little more off balance, it also applies a multi-directional force to their extended elbow. The elbow is not a strong joint, it can be hyper-extended very easily, so please practice with care.

If you want to practice the position at first, you can also work this technique from a cross-body push. If you want to work with more speed, B only lightly touches the punching hand, don't pin it to the chest. In this way, A's arm should be knocked away by the movement rather than broken!

There's a few principles at work here. There's the obvious leverage against the joint. But also think of B's acceptance of the push or punch, of blending with it. Think, also of the shoulder wave that provides the power. This can be long, or it can be applied short and sharp.

Leverage can be applied to the elbow in other positions. We have so far applied pressure to the side and upwards. Obviously

## PRESSURE POINTS

At one time, pressure points were the subject of great awe and mystery in mainstream martial arts. Some systems, particularly the Chinese internal arts were, according to some, built on an ancient knowledge of the human body's natural energy system. In the early 90's I spent some time studying aspects of this work, with various results and conclusions. *Dim mak* became fashionable and a host of "instant masters" appeared, many of whom had little direct experience in the source material. Instead, they relied on a few show piece knock outs, always on their own willing students, to promote their systems. A shame, as the whole field became tarnished with the same brush, and I have met one or two individuals who were able to produce genuine effects on anyone who cared to put themselves forward. The downside for me there was that you needed to invest a lot of time training in those people's systems, which also came with other aspects that I was not so interested in.

So how does Systema approach this subject? From my experience so far there are two aspects to pressure points from the Russian perspective. The first is physiological - we know that there are nerve points in the body that can be accessed. Anyone who has hit their funny bone can tell you that! The second is recognising that alongside the physiology is psychology. The human body is subject to the workings of

from an arm-bar we can apply pressure to break the elbow. A grabs or punches to different parts of the body and from different angles. See how each time you can "accept" the incoming force and attack the elbow. Consider how you can use the knee or even foot to apply the break in some positions.

The knee is equally vulnerable, more so if it gets locked in place by our own weight. Revisit the knee attack methods we discussed earlier. It should be easy to see how the lock becomes the break again. Let's take a specific example.

A feeds a straight punch into B. B deflects the punch and at the same time stamps down into A's knee. The kick should be powered through, more like a stamp than a kick. If needs be, B can grab and pull A forward, to make sure that the lead leg is fully loaded.

the mind and imagination, be that through fear, tension or other mechanism. We shall talk more in this in a later chapter.

Incidentally, I have included this work in the chapter on friendly work as it is often claimed that through PP's we can subdue a person very easily, almost gently and without the need for violence. It is certainly a view beloved of anyone prosecuting a martial artist in court! As trained people it seems we are supposed to have the power to effortlessly control a raging hulk with just some thumb pressure to a vital point. I'm not denying the possibility and I'm by no means condoning use of excessive force on anyone but that view is largely a falsehood and cliché from watching too many movies. Having said that, the use of points can be handy in situations where we just need to give someone a little encouragement without the risk of any injury or damage. Context is key, as always!

For now we will focus on those nerve points and how they can be used to assist in our work. Again, there is the caveat that levels of pain tolerance vary, not only from person to person but also according to the situation. Drugs, mental state and so on will all influence the amount of pain felt. Another thing to consider is the question of surprise. We find in training that when a person is aware they are about to be pinched somewhere, for example, they can to a large extent resist the pinch. The mind-body is prepared for it. When the pinch comes a surprise the body response is usually more "honest." Something to bear in mind when practicing these methods! We will also include some places are that are not nerve points, as such, but are vulnerable areas.

Let's start from the head down. I'm not going to present a complete chart of points here, but will show you the ones that I have found most useful for me and also from some of our guys who use Systema in their professional capacity.

The head and neck are both rich in points which can work well to assist with head control. The eyes are obvious weak points and any pressure applied to them will almost always result in movement away from that pressure. If a person has you pinned to a wall but your hands are free, bring both hands up to rest on the sides of their head and apply light force to the eyes with your thumbs. As you do so, add in a little rotation to further break the structure.

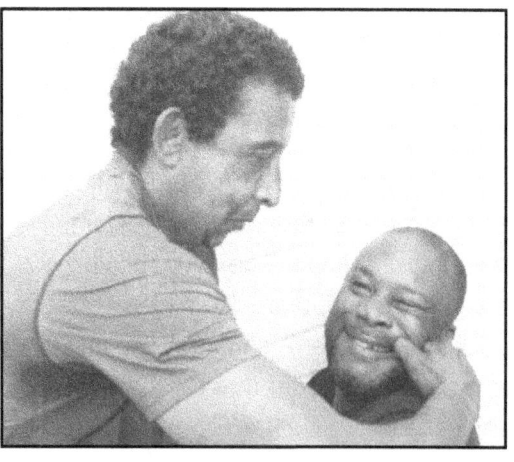

There are a couple of points around the mouth / cheeks that are useful. The first is the mouth itself, with the good, old-fashioned fish hook. If you can grab into the cheek itself, you don't always have to put your thumb in the mouth, which has obvious dangers. Pinch the cheek and pulling or rotating sharply usually does the trick.

The other point is just under the cheekbones at the root of the upper molars. Place a finger and thumb on your cheekbones, then slide down until you find it. Slight pressure will feel uncomfortable. Pressing here can affect one end of trigeminal nerve, sometimes known as the "toothache nerve." Practice this a lot and you will find out why! This is usually accessed by placing a hand across the lower face in a C grip and squeezing in and up as little. Use the elbow to direct the head up and back. Once tilted, the elbow pushes down for a takedown.

Even just covering the nose and mouth can help with direction and control. We know that the nose makes a good lever, here were are adding the concept of "sealing the breath" for good measure. A person usually naturally moves away in order to be able to breathe again.

The ears make great handles and there is also a nice nerve point just behind the ear. Place your thumb there and slide it back to just behind the jaw. Press in and you should feel it. Push in and up on this to lift someone. If

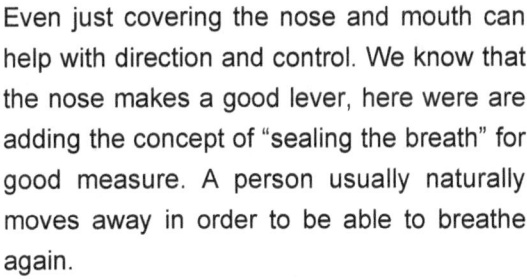

 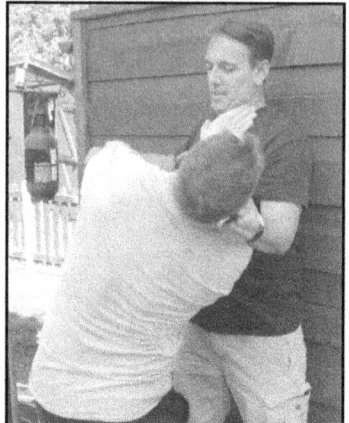 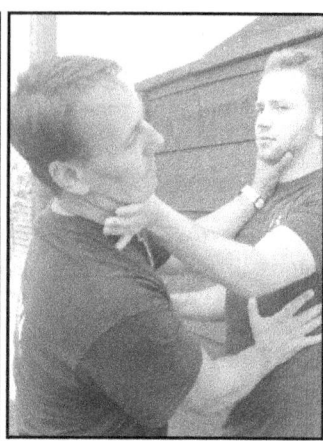

grabbing the ear, there is a method that works best. Place your had over the ear, then curl your fingers in behind it for a strong grip. To move, do not pull from the hand but work from the shoulder or hips. Add in rotation at the same time.

Let's work down to the neck, now. We have good targets on front, sides and back. The brain stem at the base of the skull, where it meets the spine, is a very vulnerable area. A sharp tap to this spot usually causes the shoulders to hunch up, as if to protect the area, so breaking a person structure and/or causing them to relax.

At the front we have another vulnerable point, the trachea. We spoke earlier of flicking with the finger into this spot to get a flinch reaction. Of course you can also hit into it with the edge of the hand or the webbing between finger and thumb. This should be a sharp tap as we want the person to move, not to damage the trachea.

Another option is to work into the notch just below the windpipe. We access this by pushing into the shoulder with the fingers. Have A walk towards B. B pushes into the opposite shoulder, which should turn A a little in towards the thumb. The thumb now

presses in and down into the clavicle notch Be firm but not forceful, with direction coming from the elbow.

Another area from the front is to work into the carotid sinuses. You can locate these by gently pushing the thumbs in the sides of the mastoid muscles. I say gently because you should be aware that some people are hyper-sensitive to CS stimulation. When triggered in such a way, the CS sends a signal to the brain that the blood pressure is too high. The brain responds by immediately dropping the blood pressure, which causes a person to

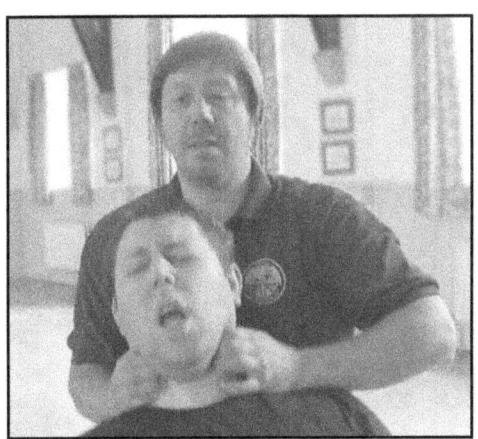

faint. In fact, we had one chap knock himself out by tapping his own CS! So go slow and feel for the points - your partner will let you know! Press in and up to lift your partner.

In use, you can grab into these points to pull someone back and down. Of course, your are also hooking into the mastoids, which provide a nice handle for work too. Curl the fingers into the grip as we did for the ear and for clothing.

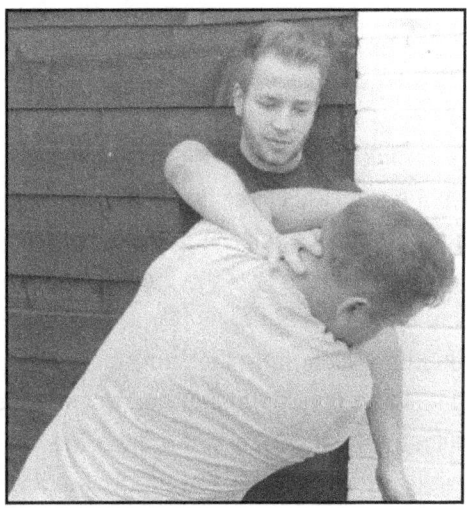

You may find you can work into the side of the neck at the base, where it meets the shoulder. Push in and down to move your partner. Alternatively, you can go full Spock and grip into the traps, just where they run out from the neck. The fingers curve in around the back of the muscle and the thumb grips and pushes in and down into the gap between muscle and collarbone. This spot has always been a bit all or nothing for me. People I've tried this on

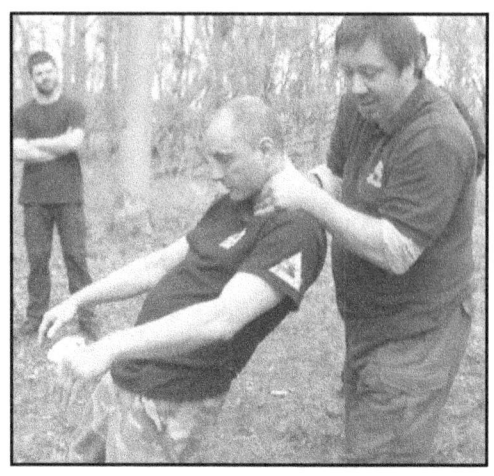

either shrug it off or collapse in agony, there's been very little in-between!

We will finish the head/neck with a takedown from the rear. This uses that brain stem fear we spoke about earlier. Again, practice with caution as this is one of the most vulnerable spots on the human body. Place the hands around the neck from the rear and use the thumbs to push up, in and then down. This will lift the head a little, then bring the chin forward so that the person collapses down into themselves. This must be a three dimensional movement, don't just push down. The hands pull the shoulders back a little as the thumbs lift. Try and you will soon get the feel of it.

There are a few points on the arm, the most useful I have found is just inside the elbow. Cup someone's elbow in your palm, then curl your fingers around the outside. About where your middle finger ends you will find a nerve point. Curve your finger into it in a hooking motion, your partner should feel some pain. We use this point to break grips. Say a person has grabbed you by the throat, swing your opposite hand to under the elbow, grab the point and pull down and to the side. It;s a good mechanical move but the nerve point should reinforce it.

Moving down into the body, there are a few easy to access points. The solar plexus is an obvious one, being a large cluster of nerves, as well as giving us access to the diaphragm. A sharp tap here will usually fold a person forward.

Slide the hands round to the sides and you'll find another point on the ribs. This is where two nerves cross. Poke around with your thumb and you'll find it. For use, strike each side sharply with the edge of the hand, or dig in with the knuckles. This works well when your attacker's arms are raised as the sides will be tense. Take care if striking your partner, it is easy to crack a rib here.

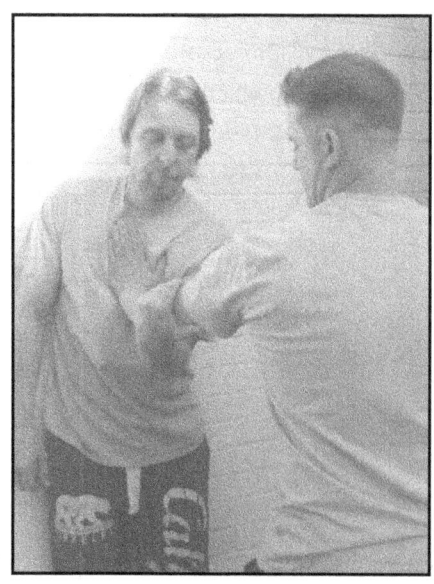

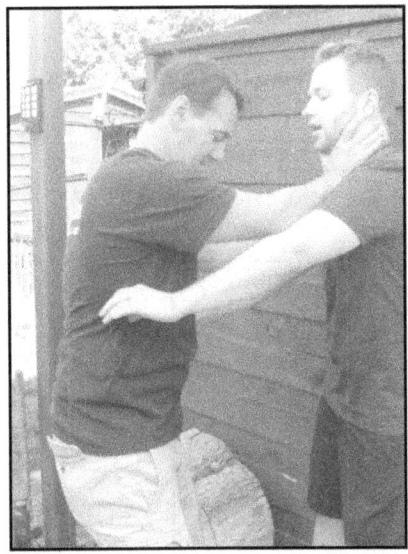

the front to take a person down. The movement must be firm and direct. In effect, you are pushing the pelvis back over the point of balance then directing it down.

Everyone knows the dead leg point. Stand upright with arms at sides. The outer point is about where your middle finger rests. But there is a corresponding point on both the inside and the rear of the thigh here too. These are easily accessible with a knee or, if you are changing height, an elbow or punch. A good hit here relaxes the entire leg and so disrupts balance.

Other points to consider on the body are the kidneys and liver for striking, the flanks for grabbing and twisting, which we will show in the next chapter.

For the lower body, the groin is an obvious target - sometimes to obvious and so well guarded. A good way to access the groin is a quick flick strike with the back of the hand. It doesn't have to be that hard, often the sharpness of the movement will cause a flinch and a corresponding relaxation or leaning forward of the body.

Another point to consider is inside the hip, the inguinal crease. There is a nerve point in here and it is also a weak spot from mechanical perspective. You can push into it with the edge of hand to block any leg movement. You can also thrust the fingers in and down into it from

We worked with the ankle earlier. The joint can be rolled to collapse the structure but again there are also some nerve points we can use here. A sharp toe kick to the inside area just above the bone will hurt!

So that's a quick guide to some of the more useful nerve points. Always remember that these are the icing on the cake, so to speak, and should always be supported by good structure, position and movement. If they, or anything else, is not working, be ready to switch into something else immediately.

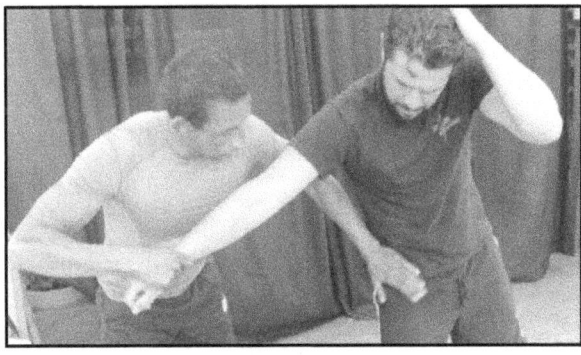

# CHAPTER TEN
# ESCAPES

An important part of learning to apply locks is also learning how to escape them. Once people are through the basics, this also gives us a nice way of working back and forth rather than just putting a hold on a static partner. As before, we could present a long list of specific techniques against specific holds. We will give you some techniques but again you should drill these as a method of learning the underlying principles, not as set moves to used in a very particular situation. For those underlying principles, we need look no further than our four pillars, with a couple of additional ideas. So we will first start with some drills to develop the pillars, then look at applying those into escape drills.

## THE FOUR PILLARS

We have already discussed the importance of breaking structure in applying restraint or throws. If we can maintain our optimum structure - spine straight, shoulders over hips, feet under hips - then we can more easily resist locks and throws. One way to practice this is as follows.

A places a hand on the base of B's skull. They use gentle pressure to move B forward. In other words, B follows the direction and speed of A's push. B should relax the body but attempt to keep the spine straight at all times. The force from the push should be transmitted directly down to the feet. At intervals, A changes the

direction of their push. They can do this by moving the hand to the side of the head. Movement throughout should be smooth and not too fast to start. The aim for B is to maintain good form as they move around.

If you find this difficult to achieve. Here is another drill you can try. Work the same drills as above, but this time B has a stick across their shoulders with their arms draped over it. This forces B into "good posture."

In the above drill we are primarily using footwork to negate incoming force and maintain posture. Another option is to use selective tension. This is where we tense or "strengthen" one part of the body, while every other part remains relaxed. Think back to the drill where A was trying to break B's posture. This time, B can resist. The set up is the same. A places a hand on B's chest and another on the lower back. A applies pressure in order to break B's structure. B applies selective tension at the points of contact in order to resist the pressure. Imagine a line of tension between the two points of contact. The resistance should match the incoming pressure and, of course, the other parts of body should be free to move. Once you have the idea, A can apply pressure in different places and directions. At this stage, pressure should be applied gradually with no sudden changes of direction, particularly if working against the neck.

Let's now work the same principle to the joints. A extends a hand and allows B to put on a simple wrist lock. Now start again, this time A applies tension into the hand and wrist. Do this by extending the fingers forward and activating the tendons rather than tightening the muscles. Push forward a little into B's movement and it should become much more difficult for the lock to be applied.

The main principles being applied here are the ideas of internal connection and support. We will describe this a little later on. For now, extend out and rotate a little, imagine your forearm is like a thick branch. You can work the same principle with B applying pressure to the inside or outside of the elbow. This type of work was the basis for many "un-bendable arm" demonstrations in martial arts. It's simply a

question of extension and tendon activation rather than anything mystical. Once again, for learning purposes, B makes no sudden changes in speed or direction. Once you have the feel, apply the same work to the feet and legs.

That's two ways to work with posture and tension. Let's now look at using relaxation and movement. We will work the same starting drills, with A applying pressure on two places. This time, instead of resisting the pressure, B yields to it and "slips out" from the push. B should feel the direction of the stronger hand and go with it. Use the other hand as a pivot. For this drill, B can break posture if required but should work back into optimum posture as quickly as possible.

Once you have worked the body, go on again to the joints. Work the wrist lock as before. This time, as soon as you feel the lock coming on, relax and rotate away. Repeat with the feet and legs.

After running through all those drills, add in a little movement. A now works continuously as B moves to escape the locks. At this stage we are working as the lock is applied. Remember, we are still at learning stage so keep things even. This time, the person being locked can apply structure / tension or movement / relaxation to escape. You can even work both at the same time if working against two attackers.

As you begin to apply more movement, you might find yourself getting occasionally stuck or caught. First check your footwork. It is very easy, especially if working tension, to plant the feet, so always make sure you are stepping enough. The second thing is to check that you are getting back to optimum posture. It is sometimes easy to escape one lock, only to place ourselves in a bad position for the follow up move. The third thing, of course, is to constantly monitor your breathing and level of psychological tension - do not allow yourself to become flustered or irritated.

If you are still getting caught a lot after that, ask your partner to slow down a little. If you are not getting caught at all, ask your partner to speed up! At some stage you will likely get caught and put into a lock. So let's next look at escaping from a hold that is on.

This time, we allow our partner to actually apply a lock and then work to escape. All of the above principles apply of course - we can work our structure, we can work movement, we can apply resistance. There are a few other concepts to look at too.

## WEAK POINT

The first is the structure of the lock itself. Consider some grabbing your wrist. If we look at the hand we see a C shape. This means that the weakest part of the grip will

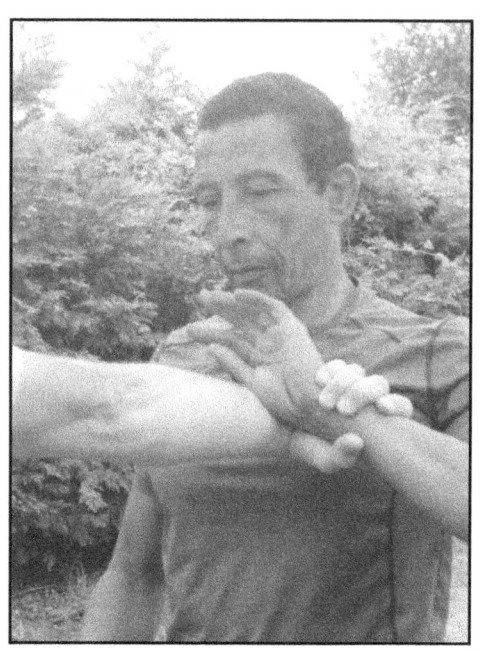

structure. Reset and this time B moves the opposite way, into the gap at A's hand. It should be easier to escape. Now try once more. This time B drops down into the space under the arm.

Of course you can work the same against a bear-hug or any other hold. Look at the shape and work towards the space. Remember to work easy at first, give your body a chance to learn.

## ONE JOINT UP

What if the hold is so strong we cannot work out of it? One approach is not to work at the point of contact but to go "one joint up."

be in that open section. Likewise in a choke - there is not only an opening at the hand end of the arm, there is also space above and below the arm. We can use two simple methods to work this principle. Keep this holds light at first, they are purely to learn a principle.

A grabs B's wrist. B relaxes and twists out of the grip working into the gap. Do not struggle, keep the movement smooth. B can work from the arm, or can simply step away to break the grip

A places an arm in choke position over B's shoulder. B should first move into A's elbow crease and try to escape that way. It should prove difficult as B is working into the strongest part of A's

A grabs B elbow firmly. Rather than try and pull the arm away. B simply goes one joint up and rotates the shoulder in order to draw A off balance. The same principle works against a wrist grab. A grabs B's wrist with a strong grip. B is unable to twist out., so works from the elbow. B rotates the elbow up and around, bringing it over A's arm to break the grip. Note that the escape is still

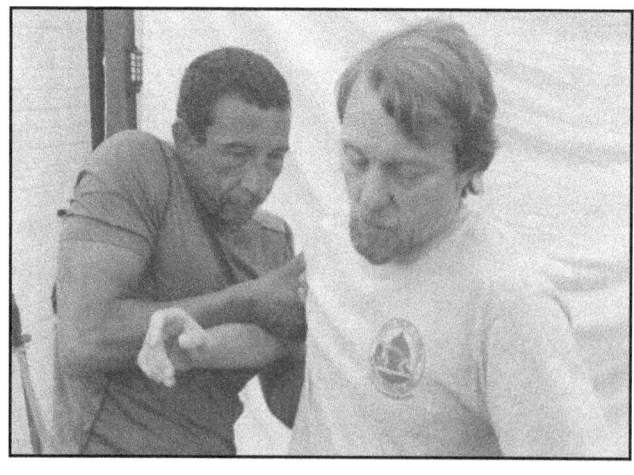

through the weak point in the C but this time B's movement is generated from another part of the body. Using this method is very good for working counter-locks too.

Another way to train this concept is for A to grab B's chest. Rather than work at the point of contact again, B can go "one joint up" to the head. B drops and ducks the head through the gap between A's arms, then bobs the head back up. Step at the same time. This should either break the grip or at least loosen it and place A in a weaker position

## SHAPE

Next time you make a cup of tea (or coffee for US readers!), observe how you reach and pick up the cup. Your fingers open to mirror the shape of the cup, your hand moves in and your fingers close around the cup. Imagine if, as you touched it, the cup changed shape. Apart from the mental shock, you might find it difficult to lift the cup. Imagine, also, if the cup was a hologram and your hand went straight through it. Either way, it's not a good start to the day!

The same applies to grabs. If a person is intent on grabbing you, their hands will from the appropriate shape. Furthermore, when they grab they except to feel some substance in their hands, some measure of what we might call density. If either the shape or the level of density is not what is

expected, the body is caught out and takes a second to adjust. That split second of adjustment is what gives us time to escape or counter. Once again, we have a couple of simple drills to help us understand this.

A walks in to grab B's wrist. B should not try and escape but should actually offer the wrist. However, as the grip comes on, B moves their arm away, in the same direction that A is walking. With the right timing, A should momentarily lose their balance, to a greater or lesser degree. The stronger A's movement and intention, the greater the effect. Think back to our foot sweep drills, it is a similar principle. And of course, once working on application we can nicely fit the foot sweep in as well!

A walks in to grab B's shoulders. As the grab is applied, B moves one shoulder back, turning their body a little, taking A with them. Again, with good timing, A will be taken off balance and positioned for a counter.

## POINT OF CONTACT

When a person has a strong grip on us, they are applying tension. We can use that tension in order to feed into our attacker's structure. We should not try and directly resist that tension but instead use rotational movement to get a result. A simple way to try this is to have A grab B's chest. B now wants A's hands to stay where they are - they may grasp A's elbows or even pin A's hands in place with their own. B next rolls and rotates their torso. Taking a step or two may also help. The effect should be that A is pulled off balance. Of course, B can work back and forward and add in a level change for a throw or takedown

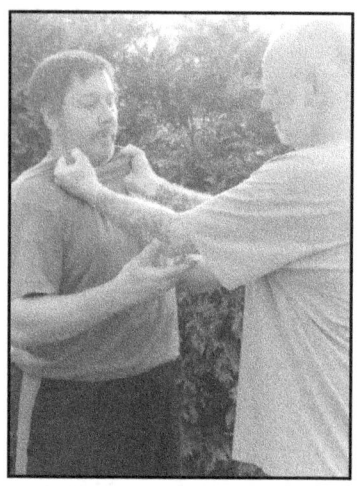

## COUNTER ELSEWHERE

If we can't work directly against the grab, or use it, we may be able to work against another part of the attackers body. Striking is an obvious way to do this but there are options. The first step to working this is to find out what parts of our body are free to move.

A applies a range of grabs to B. In each case, B allows the hold to be applied, then sees how much movement they have in the rest of the body. From there you can start to work. Here's a couple of examples.

A grabs B from round the shoulders. The grip is too strong to break, so A instead changes level, grabs A's lead leg and lifts it.

A pins B against a wall with a throat grab. B has movement in the shoulders and arms. B rolls a shoulder forward to swing a hand over, either to strike A in the face or to go into a head control movement. Note how in order to break balance, B's other hand simultaneously pulls down on A's other arm.

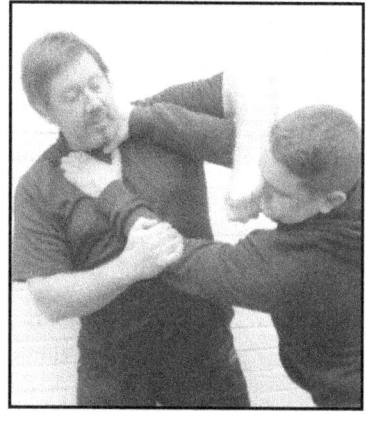

## PAIN COMPLIANCE

We can think of pain compliance as a way to get a person to move. A sharp dig in the right place can "encourage" the attacker to move away from that point. Think about it - the best way to get someone to move is to give them a strong incentive to move there, as we mentioned in our transport work.

For a simple idea, work A pinning B to the wall again. The are numerous things B can do. One thing is for B to try pinching the skin on the bottom of A's arms. Just take a small bit in each hand and pinch.

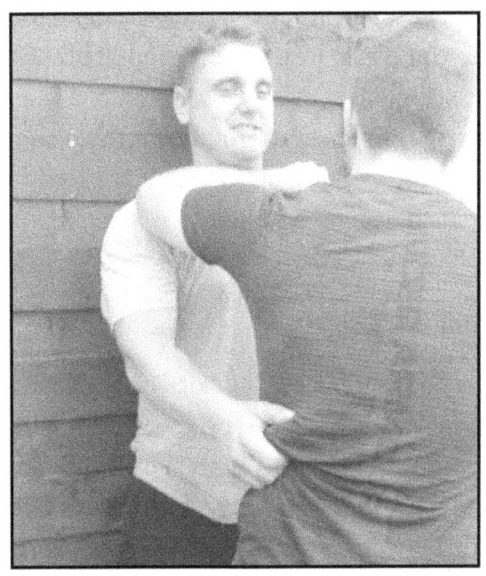

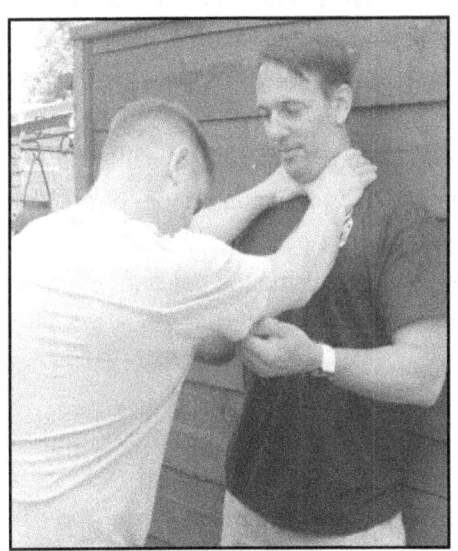

One other option for now is for B to take a handful of A's sides just below the ribs. Grab and twist one hand forward and one hand back, at the same time move forward and rotate a little to the side. As we mentioned with nerve points, when applied "out of the blue" these methods can be very effective. We also have to be aware, though, that people have different levels of pain tolerance and that might also be influenced by their mental / physiological state

These are our main escape principles, then. In reality, we may apply two or more of those in a situation, depending on the circumstances. This is why it is important to study from a principle base rather than technique. You can't cover every single possibility with a technique, but principles allow us to adapt on the fly. If a particular move is not working, don't keep doing it, you are just reinforcing failure. Instead, switch to something else.

Say you have a really strong double wrist grab. You try rotating but it doesn't work. Don't try rotating again, think about a sudden level change, or pushing forward and up or any of the other principles. Remember that using tension or structure to resist a hold is not an escape in itself, it is purely there to buy you a little time. If you keep applying resistance your attacker will likely change their movement to suit rather than hold on, get bored and give up. Use that small gap to do something else, don't get caught up in your own tension.

## APPLIED HOLDS

Having a person apply a lock or hold can be a gift or it can be a nightmare, depending on who is grabbing. By that I mean, a person who is not very skilled may grab you firmly but "lock up" their own hands in the process. There might be an incident where a drunk guy grabs you by the lapels, for example. It's easy from there to grab his ears, turn and take him down to the floor, there to be restrained or removed. In effect, he has made it easier for you to restrain him than if he was flailing around trying to hit you.

At the other end of the spectrum, if an experienced grappled gets you in a decent hold or choke, you better be very sharp and precise in your response or you are in trouble. Actually, I would say in that case, once a lock is fully on, unless you have a high skill level you will struggle to escape. Best to avoid the lock, which we will return to later on. First, we will get our partner to apply a lock and then work to escape from it using the principles above. Again, we are ruling striking out for the moment. I should also briefly mention bites and eye gouges. They've never formed part of my main armoury but they are options to be considered.

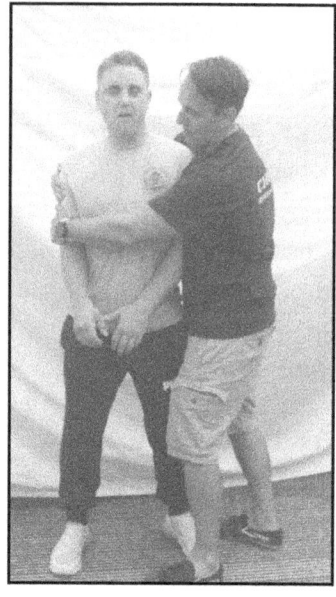

Anything may be useful when used in the right time and place but they are certainly not stand-alone techniques or "sure-fire" methods of escaping a good grappler, as some would have us believe. For a start, you still need good positioning skills in order to use them. It is also difficult to do more than simulate them in training, unless you are going to bite your training partner! So by all means consider them but only after having a good base in all the other options.

The degree to which your partner applies the lock is up to you. I'd advise a progression, so start with a loose grip and firm it up as you go along. It's impossible to cover every single type of lock and hold, instead we will run through the main body parts and look at some possible counters. Remember, always take note of the underlying principles.

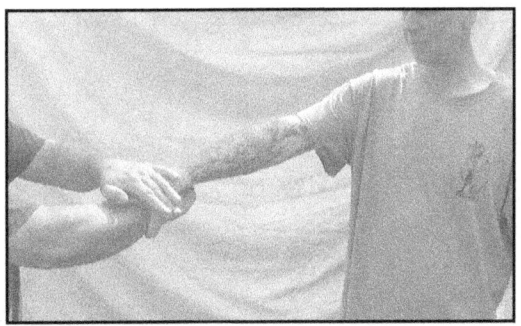
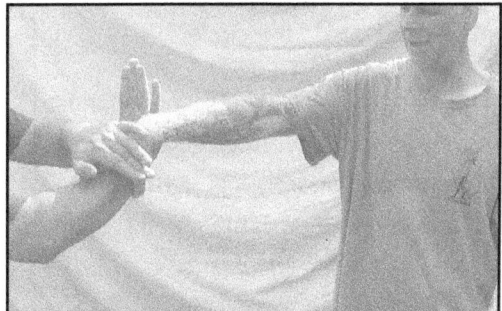

## WRIST

Single wrist grab options are to twist and escape as before, either through the use of footwork, rotation or both. If you wish to lock the other person, you can try this move, too.

A has grabbed B's right wrist with their right hand. B covers the back of A's hand with their left and rotates the right hand up and round in a clockwise direction. From here, B grabs A's wrist and applies a lock. Remember how taking a step back will help stretch A out.

If both wrists are grabbed, B turns a little and rotates their hands to thumbs up position. Continue this movement to bring the palms over A's wrists. B now sharply presses down and can also add in more turn to take A down. Remember, the power is in the movement not in tension from the arms.

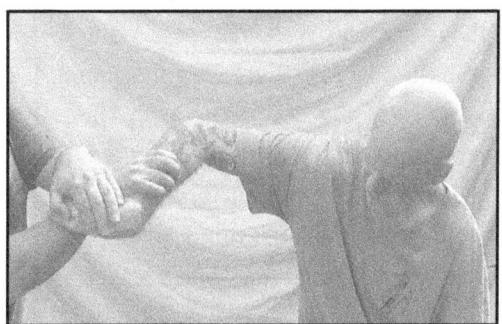

If two hands are used to grab one, consider working against another part of the attacker's body. For example, let the attacker have the wrist, then take a step back, using the contact point to pull them into head control or a similar take down.

Another double grab escape is for B to reach through with their free hand, take the fingers of the grabbed hand and pull them back and up. This should be enough to break the grip, as we are working against

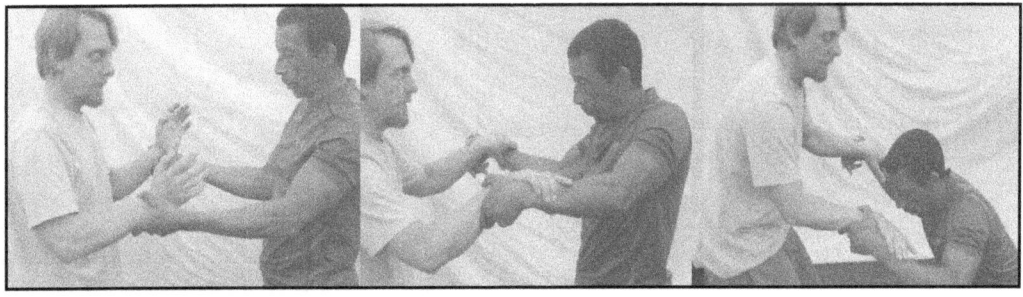

the weak point in the circle.

The same principle works if both hands are grabbed. B brings their palms together and sharply lifts them up into a "prayer" position. This should again break the grip.

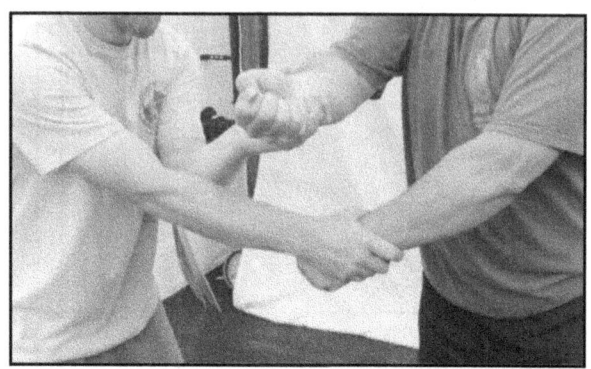

If you want to trap the attacker from the above position, work this movement. A grabs B's wrists. B crosses their right hand over the left as shown. It is important that A's arms are crossed. B next rotates their right forearm down as they pull their left hand in and up. This should have the effect of both breaking the grip.

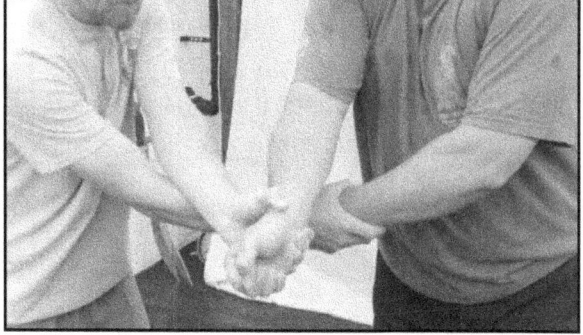

As A's right hand is pulled in, B should now bring their own right hand in so that A's arm is trapped against the body. See how A is also pulled off balance. You may find that sometimes you can trap both of A's hands this way. Finally, B pulls their left hand free and can use it to strike, control, or whatever they wish to do.

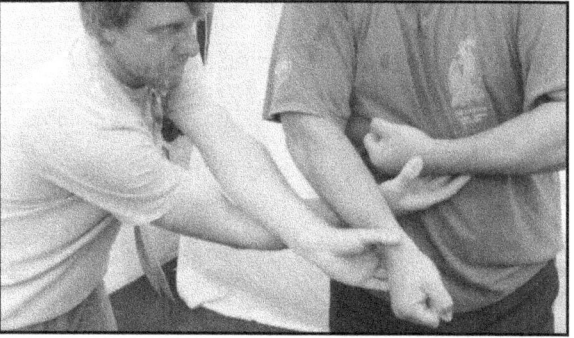

### ARM

We've already shown one way to reverse an arm bar, here's a couple more ideas. A applies the arm bar to B, who immediately steps across A's base with the nearest leg. B can now pull A forward to trip or throw them over the leg.

The gooseneck can be a painful hold but it

is quite simple to escape if we think about the triangle principle. A applies to hold to biting point - and a bit more if you like! B simply flicks their fingers up with the other hand, so changing the triangle shape and slipping out of the hold.

## CHOKE

Let's look at some choke escapes now. As mentioned, these are the most dangerous and you need to work very quickly in order to escape I suggest that the holds start light and work up in strength. This is also a good way of getting some what acclimatised to being choked, or at least learning not to panic and tense up in that situation. Remember the principles of the blood and air choke, and be sure to protect the airway and sides of the neck where possible.

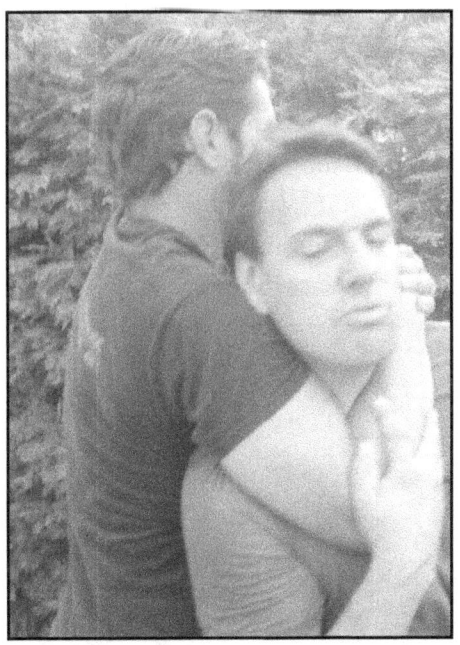

All of these methods being with A applying a single arm choke. There are two main methods we use. The first is to "grab" the choking arm and use it to throw the attacker. So as A's arm comes over to apply the choke, B grabs A's arm - that can be the clothing, muscle or into the elbow crook - and pulls sharply forward and down. At the same time, B steps out with the same leg, twists their hips and leans forward a little, to throw A.

Our second method is to work into the space available in order to escape out of the choke. To get a good feel for this, have A apply a loose single arm choke. B takes both arms out to the sides. They next drop the shoulder under the choking arm and make a big circle with

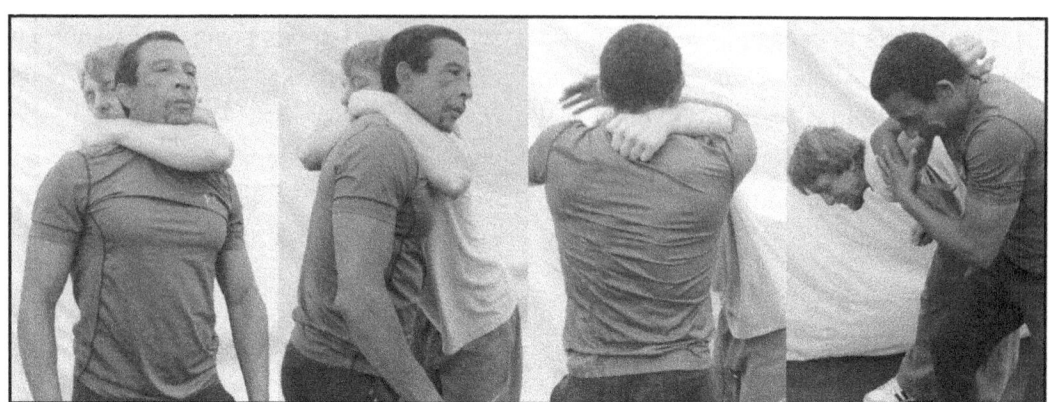

the arms by turning the body. It is important that you turn from the waist, taking a step or two as you do so. This will have the effect of creating space under the choking arm and then moving you into it, using the power of the turn. So that is the principle, let's look at a few more applications.

A applies the choke to almost full on, let's say over B's left shoulder. B immediately drops that shoulder and turns into the choke. As B turns, they bring their own right arm up and over to place A in a shoulder lock. The trick again is to really drop the shoulder to create space and use the power of the hips to turn the body. Think of the body as a pendulum, the top part is fixed but the lower part can "swing".

Depending on the feel of the situation it is also possible to turn out of the choke. In this case, the choke comes on over the right shoulder, so B drops the left shoulder and turns. B can also grab the wrist and pull it down a little to loosen the hold. Make sure not to bend too far forward, or you may make the situation worse! Use the power of the hips again. At the same time, B brings their left hand up onto B's face. B then straightens from the hips, rotating A's head back into a take down.

The techniques so far rely on having some mobility in the shoulders. For the next method, you will need very relaxed shoulders. A applies the choke over the right shoulder. B places the outside of the thumb

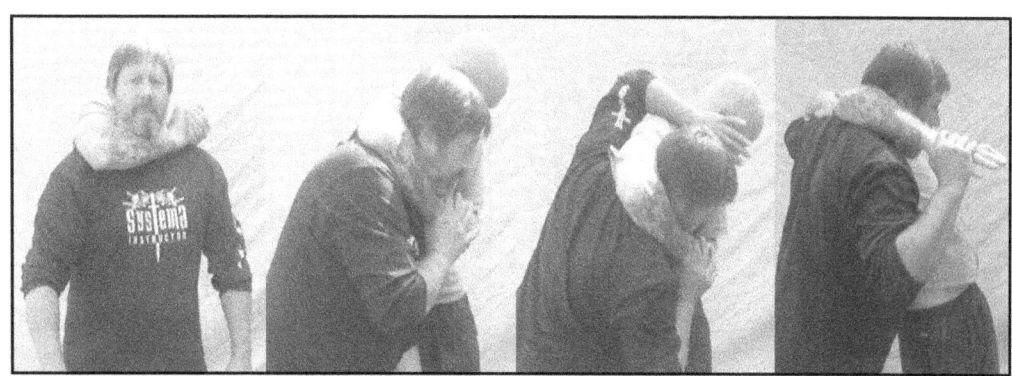

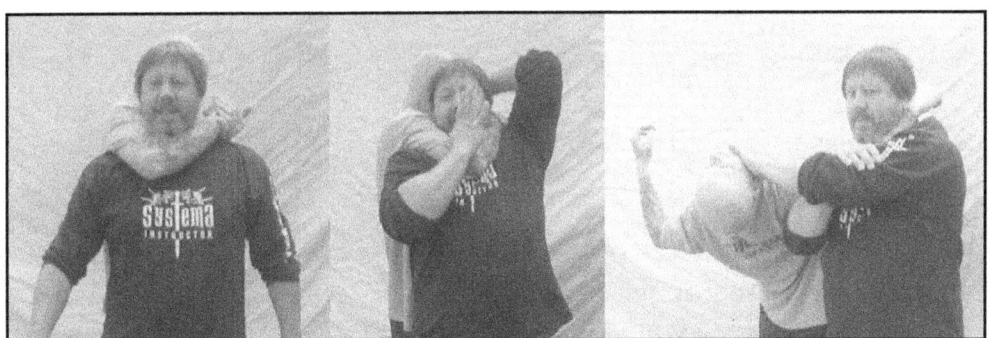

into A's elbow crease and pulls/rolls the hand sharply down to create space. At the same time, B's left hand reaches over and back onto a's face. B next drops the right shoulder and rotates out from the hips, bringing their right hand to their left bicep. This should escape the choke and bring a lock onto A.

If A is standing a little more to the side, another option is for B to bring both hands up to grab A's head. The hands go either side, or to the face and back of the head. B now rotates the head and pulls down and to the side. This should bring A down to the floor.

If a person applies a choke and pulls you back, off balance, you have to work very quickly. Think back to our first technique where the arms come out to the sides. Repeat this, at the same time one foot steps back behind the other. If you are turning to the right, the right foot steps back. This should help maintain balance and also make your twist stronger. Again, your movement needs to be quick and decisive.

So far we have looked at single arm chokes. Let's finish for now with a double arm choke, the sleeper hold. This is a much is a stronger grip so you must work quickly. You may be able to work the shoulder drop methods, or you can try this technique. A applies the sleeper, right arm choking, left arm behind the head. B should tuck their chin in to the left in order to protect the throat. At the same time they quickly bring their left hand up to push on A's left elbow. Next, B grabs A's left wrist with their right hand. From their, B applies an arm-bar using the head as a fulcrum. B can apply a break or turn and drop to spin A out to the side.

Again I would stress that the success of these techniques depends very much on you having relaxed, mobile shoulders, turning the body as a unit and working before the choke fully bites. The longer you leave it, the more difficult your escape. There are other techniques too, but they tend to be variations on these methods. Play around with the principles and you will find them.

A variation on chokes are guillotine and full nelson holds. The former are chokes applied in a bent position. It's often a common tactic in a brawl for people to grab someone around the neck and pull them forward into this position. The aim is not so much to choke, though that is possible from here, as to rag the other person about a bit or to punch them in the face with the other hand. Let's look at a couple of basic escapes.

A has grabbed B round the neck and pulls them forward. B has gone with the movement a little but manages to keep as upright as they can. The next part of this move is something we used to call "Testicles, Spectacles!" B taps A in the groin with the far hand (the right in this case.) The strike should bring a forward slightly. B immediately brings their other hand up onto A's face. B now uses the power of the hips

to straighten up the body, at the same time rolling A's head back and down. This should have the effect of breaking the grip. Working into the eyes another option but should not replace the rotation part of the move.

An option is for B to bring their closest hand across to A's shoulder. Thins hand pulls back and down as B pushes sharply into the back of A's knee with their own. The aim is to twist A to the floor. Again, B should use the power of the hips for the movement.

From the same position it is also possible to go forward. In one version, B brings their hand onto the shoulder as before. This time, B drops away from A, pulling on the shoulder as they go. The idea is to use the bodyweight to unbalance A, then throw them on the fall. B could also place their other hand on A's nearest knee in order to block any movement from it and top assist with the unbalancing.

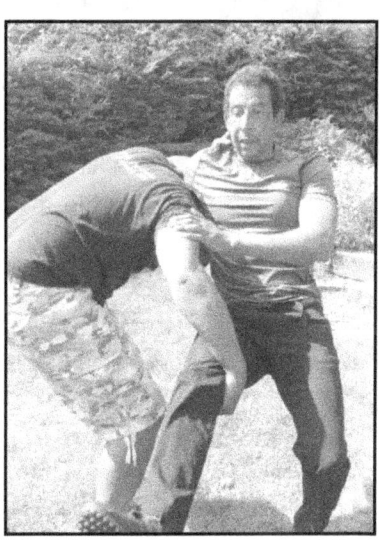

A variation on this movement is for B to go into a forward roll. As A pulls them forward, B follows the movement, drops and rolls. As they do so, the opposite arm circles up to go between A's legs. This becomes a joint strike/lift to the groin. It is important that B lifts A over them as the go in order to throw them - otherwise there is a risk A will land on top of B.

If the guillotine is applied from the front, the groin is an obvious target. B could also try pushing back to lock A's lead knee, or lifting the lead leg in order to take A back. Be aware, though, that a fear of falling may cause A to tighten their grip.

We'll next look at bear-hugs. If caught tight, see what parts of the body are free to move. In this case the hips and legs can work. So B steps round behind A's leg, then straightens up using the power of the hips to push the knee forward and the elbow back, scissoring A off-balance.

Another option is to bend and twist, with the aim of throwing the attacker away. From a forward bend it may also be possible for B to grab A's leg, then straighten up form the hips, so tilting A back. You may also be able to lock the knee from this position.

Sometimes a person applies a bear-hug then tries to lift us, The easiest way to prevent the lift is to wrap our leg around the attackers - though this does limit our options for escape.

If we think about the shape of the hold. We can see that an obvious escape route is down. So if B is quick enough they may also drop as A applies the bear-hug.

A full nelson is a strong move and can be difficult to shift once

it is fully on. One method is for B to work against the weak points in A's structure - the inter-linked fingers. To do this, B expands the

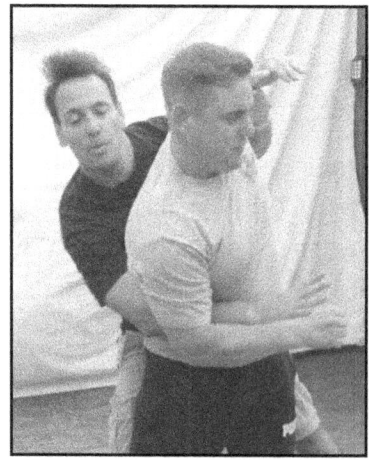

chest, squeezing the shoulder blades together. Next, relax the chest and push the back out. Use this move to power the arms. Explosively push one hand down and the other elbow up and back. Twist the waist at the same time. Imagine you are punching with one hand and hitting back with the other elbow.

Some of the same escape methods can be used as against the bear-hug. The step round, for example and also the body drop.

There are many other types of hold but I hope that, at this stage, the techniques described here will give you some ideas on how to apply our basic principles. Of course, the best way to escape a hold is to not let it come on in the first place. That may mean taking evasive action as someone is moving towards you, creating space to escape. In another situation, where you have to deal with the person, you may want to let them just grab, in order that they are committed to the attack, and then act. The key is timing - don't let the grip fully bite.

One example of this would be defence against a double leg take down. If you wait

until it's on, you are already on the floor! So as the person comes in, place both hands on their back, slide your legs back and drop your full weight into them. There are other methods, of course, but this is a very simple one to do, if you get the timing right.

In many ways, the best defence against grabs is to strike, though that may not always be the most appropriate action. A good start point to train this is to have your partner apply a deep hold and maintain position. Now place your fist, foot, elbow, etc somewhere on their body and push. This will teach you the right places and angles in which to strike. You should be able to move your partner with little effort. From there, progress to placing the strike just as the hold is coming on. See how you can hide your strike by working inside your partner's movement. We will describe this in more detail later on.

We will finish this chapter by looking at an even more challenging situations - having two people hold you. Again, we apply our work at different stages of the situation.

The first drill is for A and B to grab and C to escape. The aim here is for C to move away from the lock as soon as they see it coming or as soon as they feel it touch. C can also consider working tactically. So as they evade A's grab, c moves into a position that makes it harder for B to grab them. This brings us to the concept of shielding.

This is simply where we use a person or people as a shield. It may be visually, such as in our earlier pair Chain movement, or if we are hiding in a crowd. In this drill C uses

A or B to block the other's movement, as in the picture below. This can be a one off movement, or C might keep contact and control, actually moving A/B around with them. In this case, think of all the earlier balance points and movement handles we spoke about.

From there, C can work a little later, waiting for the holds to take a slight grip before responding. They can now begin to work on our second important concept when dealing with multiples - joining them together. Let's say A and B have both has grabbed C by the shirt front. If C ducks under one arm and turns, they will cross A/B's arms over. Pressing down on the top arm will affect both, in much the same way as we worked before against two people fighting each other.

The final stage is for C to allow the A/B holds to come fully on. This is much more challenging so I suggest at first A/B apply the holds then remain static. C should apply all our previous principles - look for the weak point in the holds, see what space they can move into, see what parts of the body they can move and so on. Consider using wave movement to bring A and B together, or changing level and so on. You can then have A/B become more active in the attempts to restrain, see again how C can bring the two of them together and work on them as one unit.

To conclude, a fun drill is to have the whole group grab and escaping - everyone for themselves or ganging up on someone else! This helps keep people lively to both escaping and also not tying themselves up too much when locking another person.

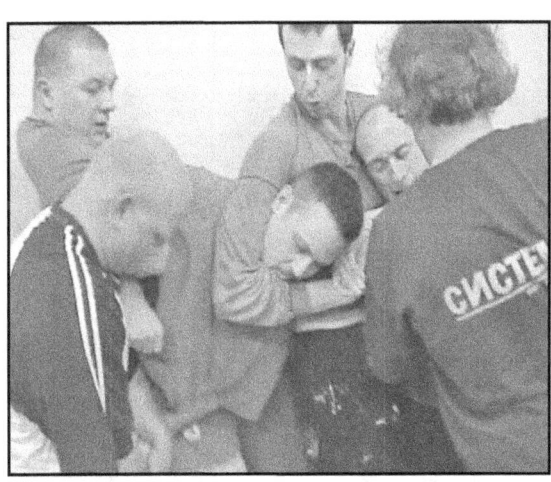

# CHAPTER ELEVEN
# PROGRESSION

One way that people measure progression in martial arts is by the complexity or difficulty of the technique being carried out. The Systema approach is somewhat different but is there value in learning more complex techniques? I think there can be, depending on how and why we do so.

Firstly, we can use this type of work to challenge our existing capabilities, to encourage us to explore our full range of movement and to be creative and bolder in our movement. Secondly, any increase in complexity can also help develop our attributes - our co-ordination, sensitivity, and so on.

The important thing is that more complex work does not replace our "bread and butter" methods and we always keep an eye to practicality. Any skills gained should be easily transferable to our regular work. We should always bear in mind how we react under pressure. There is a school of thought which claims that under stress even trained people drop to a primitive level of skill, where only the grossest motor actions are possible. This flies in the face of all the evidence. Consider fighter pilots, racing car drivers, concert pianists, surgeons and a whole host of other activities. Now, of course, if you are dropped straight into a stormy ocean having never swum before, you are likely to encounter difficulties! But if you have been trained in a progressive, layered way to deal with fear and tension stress and understand how to carry out activities while under stress, then the picture changes considerably. So sometimes, if a person has trained well those seemingly "complex" moves can actually be carried out with apparent ease. That is one aspect of the Systema approach.

Then, of course, we work from the base of principle. This highlights the importance of "play" in our training. We can set up drills in such a way that allow for full exploration of our capabilities, that do not just confine us to rote movement, or "he does A so I do B" responses. In musician terms, this is the difference between a person who can only play from sheet music and person who can improvise and write their own tunes. Both share certain requirements, in terms of a measure of technical ability and understanding but each is a very different mindset and interpretation, or expression. You might think of Systema a language. We don't speak in individual words so much as in phrases and sentences. The more articulate, the more fluent we are, the better we can communicate with others.

So in this chapter we will cover two approaches. The first are some more "advanced" techniques that you might like to try - with the proviso again that they are ways to get you thinking about different possibilities rather than set in stone moves. The second is to delve deeper into some of those principles we have already touched on and to begin working on a more internal level. The true progression is to make our work more subtle, more simple, more direct, to use less effort to get a bigger result. On a visual level, this is considerably less impressive and exciting to watch than a flying arm-bar. On a practical and "life" level it is the good way to go, for all sorts of reasons.

## TECHNIQUES

The following call for a good understanding of the basic technique and your own movement as they are a little more athletic than our earlier methods. Let's first look at a couple of ways to work an arm-bar from standing to ground.

A feeds in a punch to B. B deflects and control's A's wrist, while moving a little to A's outside. B next pulls A forward so the punching arm is low and A is leaning forward a little. B quickly steps over A's arm, maintaining control of the wrist.

B sits into A's body and drops to the knees, so bringing A to the floor. B makes sure to keep A's arm extended. From this position, B slides their foot under A's neck / face and rolls over onto their back. The direction of the roll is away from A's head. This should have the effect of flipping A over onto their back, from which position the full arm-bar can be applied.

Remember, when flipping a person in this way, or in any similar position, be sure to work from the hips as much as you can. Don't just try and muscle the person with your leg, think

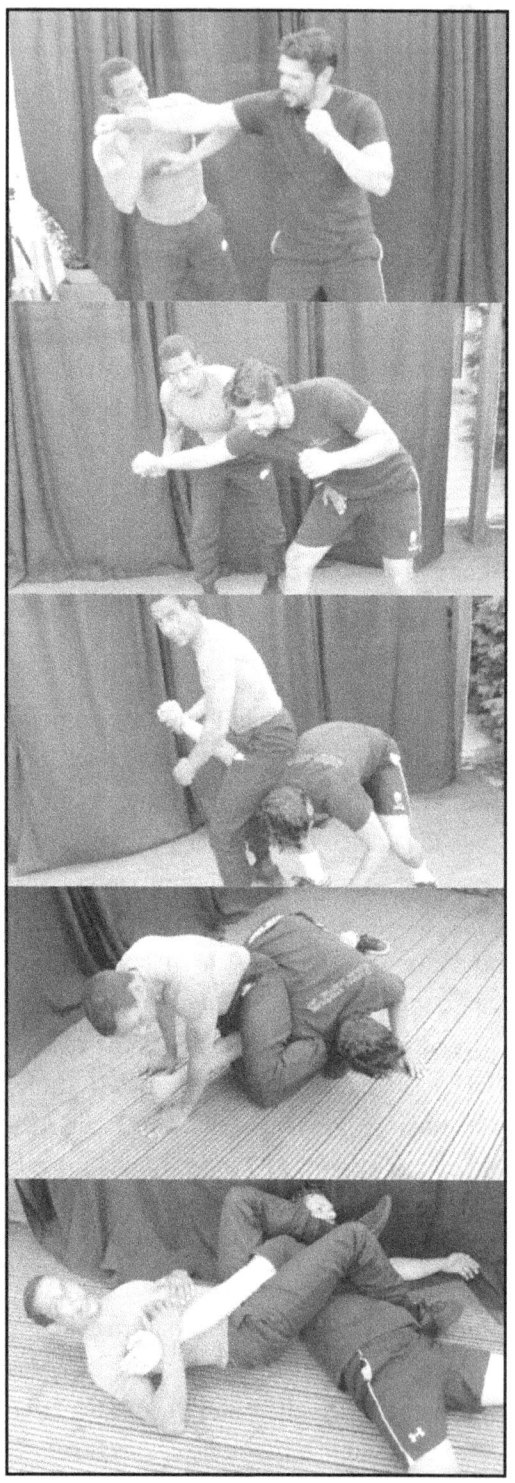

back to our wave motion.

For something even more athletic, try the flying arm-bar. There a numerous variations on this and it is a technique that's rather difficult to capture in still pictures! But let's look at a basic set up.

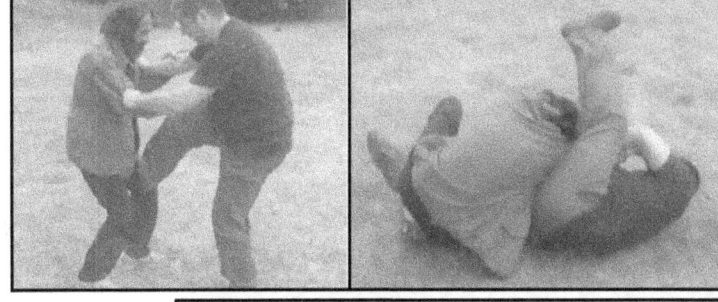

A and B are grabbing each other. To train the throw, B places their foot into A's thigh or stomach. B now sits, bringing their head close to A's foot. In this case, B has the right foot raised so they sit towards A's left pulling A forward and down.

As B falls and A comes over, B quickly swings their left foot up and over the side of A's face. From here B pushes the left leg sharply down. This should bring A down and into position to apply the arm-bar. B should make sure that they keep good control on A's other hand as they fall back. In order to maintain control of the arm.

Later on, you may wish to try kicking the first leg up and just to the side of your partner, then swing the second leg over as you are in the air. This has the effect of using your entire bodyweight to bring your partner down into the arm lock. Of course, take all due care and attention when practicing this type of move.

Once you have the idea you can experiment with different variations, all with the basic idea of attaching your falling bodyweight to your partner, then twisting as you fall.

Sudden levels changes can be used to escape and to line up a counter. A grabs B by the shoulders. B quickly drops ,the key is bringing the hands in as close to the feet as you can. As the hands touch the floor B's legs spring back to each side of A's. B can either twist from the hips, or use the impact of the legs to bring A down.

We can use a similar idea if a takedown doesn't work. A is trying to apply a throw but B is too strong for the move to work. A quickly turns to the side and drops, palms to the floor. As the upper body falls, A swings their legs up to apply the scissor takedown from the earlier chapter. Of course with any work that takes us to the floor we must be ready to work there or to get up quickly, we will look at a way of practicing that later on.

## REFINEMENTS

Another aspect of "advanced" technique is for the movements to be more subtle, rather than the overt methods above. There is a place for each, of course, and learning both helps us in many ways. Subtle techniques are useful in situations where our work needs to be "quiet." That may be in a social setting, in a close protection role or where our work is likely to be monitored and judged. Big "flashy" movements can draw a lot of attention and, to some on-lookers may appear "over the top". Nothing looks like excessive use of force than overt movements and tension.

So revisit the earlier work on takedowns and sweeps and this focus on making your movements much smaller. Focus on angles and precision. When working

directly against the body, see how you can position your hands in such a way that it is difficult for an on-looker to see precisely what you are doing. At higher levels, it almost looks as though the person throws or falls themselves, with no apparent force. As the saying goes, "the more skilled the master, the less you see."

There are a nice series of takedowns available from the simple handshake. Again, these are visually low key and may be useful in situations where you want to quickly control a person and prevent any escalation. If we approach someone with a smile and an extended hand, it is surprising how many will take the proffered handshake.

For the first one, A takes the hand and extends their fingers slightly down and out to the side. The thumb goes over the other person's thumb. From here A angles sharply down, applying pressure through B's thumb joint. This should lock the wrist, forcing B to go forward and down. Done sufficiently, you can take the other person to the floor with this movement, pull them towards you as you step back to extend them out.

Another method uses pain compliance by locking the little finger. From the handshake position, A slides their other hand underneath, peeling away B's little finger. A next locks the finger in place and applies pressure upward. This should bring tension up B's arm and into their shoulder, causing them to lift up on their toes.

For the third method, from the grip A extends their first two fingers to press into B's wrist crease. This folds the wrist and allows A to pull be forward, into head control or similar.

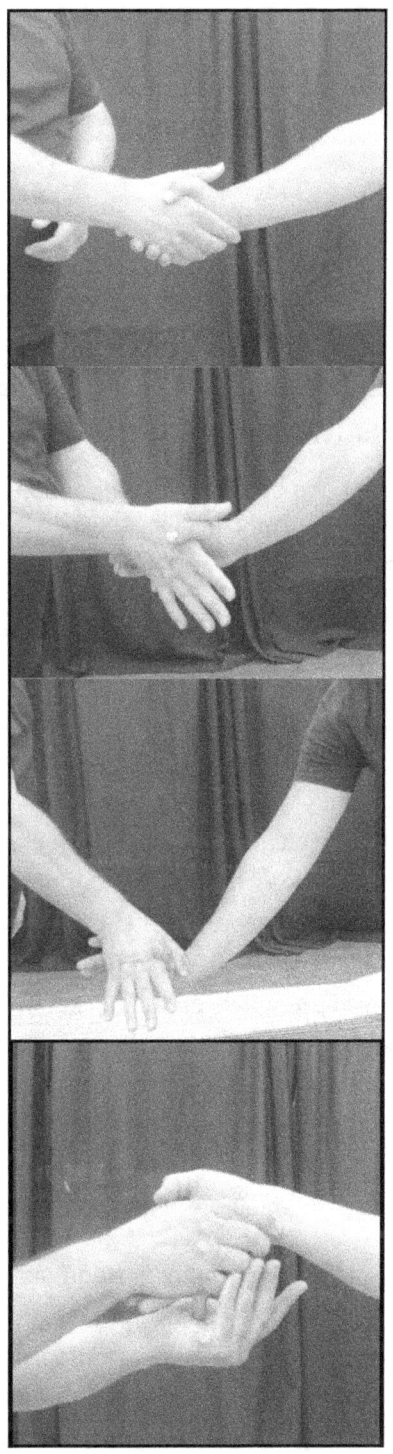

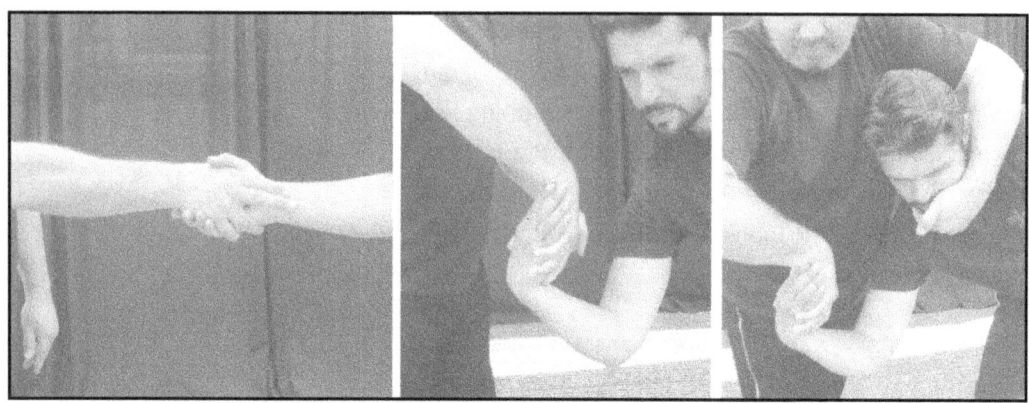

## FEAR AND PAIN CONTROL

We have spoken in earlier chapters about body structure, the use of levers and so on. These are external factors. Let's now look at some more internal factors involved in more refined work.

Breathing is the fundamental pillar of Systema work. It is its own huge topic and I point you towards many of the excellent resources available from Systema HQ and other places. In short, our breathing should always be appropriate to the task at hand. We use burst breathing to control stress levels, regular breathing to encourage smooth movement and so on. If you want to run a drill specific to locks, look back to our preparation exercise where A applies a lock on B and B has to breathe through the pain and discomfort.

To take this to the next stage, have two or more people applying locks. The full version is to have a person applying a lock to each hand and foot and a fifth person applying hits/slaps and pinches. The recipient can be standing or on the floor and should allow each hold to "bite". Of course, the people applying the locks should do so with care and caution but shouldn't be too "nice" in this drill. The aim is to cause pain (but not damage!).

There are various methods we can use to overcome the pain. The standard approach is to use burst breathing. We attempt to "breathe the pain out". Each exhale takes some pain with it and helps the body to relax. Another method is to accept the pain but to detach ourselves from it. This might mean retreating to a "happy place," in effect removing our conscious mind from the situation. An interesting thing you may find is that the pain from one part of the body in this exercise may be intense but is overcome by pain from another part.

Along with pain, or the threat of pain, comes fear. Good Systema training will equip you with all the tools you need to manage fear. Note I never say "get rid of fear." Why would we want to do that? Fear is very useful!

Anyone who tells you they feel no fear or have conquered fear is likely not being totally honest. The point is that we feel the fear but do not let it overwhelm us. In fact, we can use the fear to prompt our response. A fear reaction usually tends to be a flinch or similar, so let's start there.

.A applies the lock on B and it should be taken to a point of pain. The goose-neck hold is a good one for this. A applies the lock sharply and B has to "ride" their reaction. I suggest at first A applies and immediately releases the lock. B uses burst breathing to get rid of the pain.

The second stage is to repeat but this time B uses the Moving Tension drill we've described in other books (in brief, move the tension from the wrist, up the arm, across and out through the other hand.) This has the advantage of giving B a direction of movement and also helps "activate" the rest of the body. This should break the freeze response we can get when we experience a sudden pain.

The next stage is for A to apply the lock to cause pain and now B uses the movement generated to escape and/or counter. The feeling for B should be akin to touching a hot pan - no-one stops to think about it, the hand is immediately snatched away.

Another way to use our fear is to work it from a visual stimulus and the anticipation of pain. A and B grab C by the arms. At first it can be a simple grab. Later you can work into more involved holds. We now need a fourth person, D, who comes running in to deliver a strong kick to C. This should be a very clear movement and full of intent. The idea is to scare C so much about the kick that they escape the holds and move out of the way

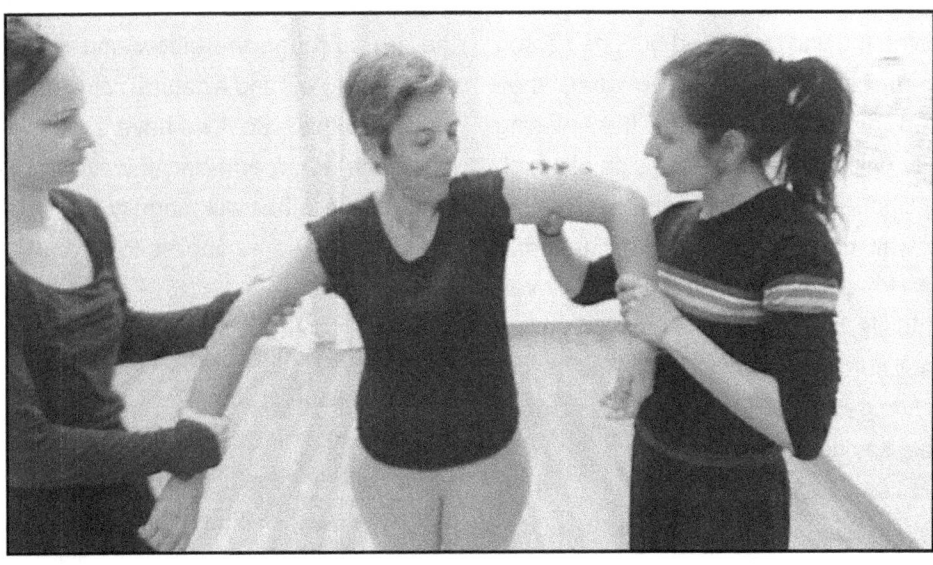

without thinking about it. In other words, the fear of impact overrides the dear of the holds. So it does mean that D has to try and instil a genuine fear in C.

You may wish to try other ways to do this. One we found works very well is a bit of dog's mess on a stick, no-one wants to get touched by that! Of course you will need a dog… and a stick.

In any event, I'm sure you get the idea. As usual, you can work in numerous variations on this theme - it doesn't have to be holds even. A friend told a story about an incident from their military days. The unit came under fire in an urban setting and scattered for cover. When the problem had been resolved the unit re-formed but one person was missing. Fearing the worst, they looked around and heard the missing soldier calling from the other side of a high wall. Under fire, he had gone over a high brick wall, despite wearing all his gear and pack. However, he couldn't get back over. Eventually, his colleagues had to boost one of their number up to the top of the wall to help him get back. Fear gives us wings, as the old saying goes.

## WAVE AND CENTRE

We have already spoken a little about applying wave movement so some of our locks. Wave movement is where one part of the body initiates our movements and it ripples through the body. Think of it as cracking a whip or flicking a towel. Try it from the shoulder - circle your shoulder up and forward, allow that movement to travel down the arm, through the elbow and out of the fingers. You will find a natural spiral develops as you do this. So if we have a person in a lock such as an arm-bar, a wave from one hand to the other will magnify the effect of our lock. The same applies to throws.

A grabs B by the lapels and attempts to move them to the side using tension from the arms alone. If you a very strong you may find it easy, if the person is heavy, then less so. In either case it takes some effort to move the person. Now A tries again but this time applies a wave movement. So the right hand initiates the movement and the wave ripples across the shoulder and out of the opposite hand. A can also add in a turn of the waist and will find B is moved much easier. The human body finds it difficult to deal with incoming force from two vectors and, as we noted, the wave brings a spiral with it. From the very first contact, this should slightly off-balance your partner and

so make them easier to move - remember our tilting the wardrobe analogy from earlier. This method is easily applied to throws. A has tightly grabbed B's arm. B expands their chest out, then sinks it back in, creating a wave movement from the

chest down the grabbing arm. B can also take a small step if required. The effect should be to break the grip and/or pull A off-balance.

A more dynamic use is to have A come in with a fast grab to the shoulders / neck. B should allow the grab to come on just slightly, so that A is committed to the movements. B first goes a little in the direction of the grab, then suddenly "waves" back in the opposite direction. B can add in a step, turn and a weight drop in as well to

increase the effect. A should be thrown clear.

The wave, then, largely uses our movement to work on the opponent. It works much easier, though, if we can feel that person's centre of balance. We can sometimes see the centres but it is more of a tactile attribute as looks can be deceiving! As I sit writing this there is a wine bottle on the table (and it's only 11 am, I know!). It's three-quarters full. If I push at the base of the bottle, it slides across the table. If I push at the top, the bottle tilts. From this I can establish that the centre for the wine bottle is low down near the base. The wider the base, the firmer the balance tends to be.

Having found the centre, the next thing is to think of direction. Take the handbrake off of your car and push it. Where do you push? Sideways on the driver's door? No, you go the boot (or trunk) and push, or perhaps you push from the bonnet, right? Because forward and back is the natural direction of the car, due to the position of the tyres. We know that the same applies to people, as we have already looked at the triangle point.

Now, we combine that feeling of centre and the direction together. Go back to our basic exercise where A places a hand on B's shoulder. Before, we pushed or pulled to the triangle point, it was probably quite a large movement. Do the same again but

this time with as little force as possible. Start by resting your palm on your partner. Don't do anything at first, just feel for where the centre of balance is. If you have trouble, work from an easier position such as the centre of the chest. You should feel a point where there is less resistance even to just a light pressure. Your partner feels a little "empty" there. Now apply your direction - towards the triangle point. You should find you can move your partner with barely any pressure from you hand. In fact, this is a good opportunity to practice your wave. So initiate your push from the opposite hand, or from your feet. Get this right and your partner may even fly back some distance - so be prepared for that.

Having practiced on a static person at first, we next begin moving. A good method is for partners to stand opposite each other and push or pull on the body. You can work with different stances, wide, narrow, one foot forward. The aim is not to shove but to

capture your partner's centre in your hand. This is a feeling thing, you will know when you have it!

Next, work from arm contact. Same set up but now both forearms are touching. You can now begin to work feeling your partner's centre through their arms. Next, add in some footwork. Move around your training space but maintain contact. Finally you can add in work with the legs too, either contact or using sweeps and trips. Be careful that this doesn't devolve into a wrestling match. That is fine but it is not the purpose of this drill, we are aiming to tap into balance and direction, not just snatch and grab or use technique.

## MOVEMENT

Another aspect of direction is to tap into your partner's movement. A rests both hands on B's shoulders. Relax and feel for the centre as before but now we also feel for direction. You see, we think we are standing still but there is a lot of movement in the body. The heart beats, the lungs work, blood is rushing round the system. We are constantly making micro-adjustments to overcome gravity. If you "listen" with the hands you can feel this movement. You may feel a slight sway in your partner. Match its direction with your hands, back and forth. Gradually amplify it, be subtle. Your partner will stumble without feeling any force from you. Once you have that, repeat and direct to the triangle point.

If you don't have a partner to work with, you can begin to develop these skills with the stick balance drill from Chapter Three. Balance the stick in the palm and when it beings to fall, curl the fingers in a light grip and follow the direction of the fall. So if the stick falls to the right, I hold the stick, let it drop and take a step or turn to the right. You only move for as long as the stick is falling and you stop the stick at the bottom of the fall. For the next stage, do not stop the stick at the bottom of the fall but let it swing up

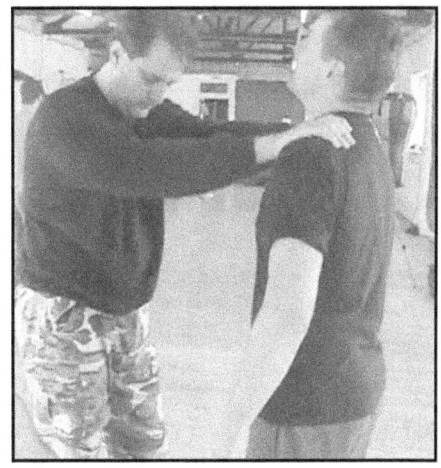

again. This gives you a new direction to follow. So now you should be taking two or so steps. You can make this a continuous move, of course, just following the pendulum movement of the stick as it goes up and down. This will get you used to the idea of following.

When you next come to work with a partner, try the same drill. A holds the stick upright and B grabs the wrist. A lets the stick fall and follows it, as before. See how this can often help you escape the grab, or at least put you in a better position to work against your partner. In effect, your partner's grab moves the stick, so you are using it as a way to amplify the feel of the direction your partner gives you.

Of course, in a dynamic situation our partner very helpfully gives us very clear movement and direction, sometimes too much! At first, we learn to use this on a gross motor level. A stands opposite B and pushes with their right hand to B's right shoulder. It should be a strong push. First few times, B can rotate and absorb the push, without stepping, just to make sure the body is relaxed. Then, B rotates away from the push as before but brings their left hand up to gently grasp A's elbow. B then takes a few steps, following the direction of the push. They should be able to lead A quite easily by the elbow.

Of course, you can also work pre-contact. The goal is to gently re-direct A's movement. A should not feel they are being pulled or led, we don't want our opponent to feel our response and so change their angle of attack. You can work this back and forth into a nice flow drill. You can then work this from different positions and with different parts of

the body. See or feel the direction of force, accept and go with it, re-directing as you do so. From here it should be easy to work in your basic locks, takedowns and throws from earlier.

As an example, A comes in with a strong shove. B connects with the pushing arm and re-directs as they turn slightly aside, bringing A forward. The re-directing hand immediately moves to A's forehead and their own forward movement causes their head to tilt, allowing B to make an easy takedown.

**INTEGRATION**

Remember our wave exercise from earlier? Now we revisit it, adding in the concepts of centre and direction to the wave. You should find your partner moves even easier. The easier it feels for you, the better you are working the concepts. Any undue strain or effort on your part means that something is going wrong. Change immediately, don't reinforce failure!

Once you can do this static, start working with movement. As before, have your partner feed in any type of attack and whatever speed you are comfortable with. Focus on feeling their centre and direction with your first touch, wherever that may be. Re-direct it or extend it along the most appropriate vector to over-balance your partner. Keep your own movements fluid and light, don't forget to breathe! Ask your partner for feedback. Can they feel what you are doing? If they can, they can begin to counter with an appropriate response.

I can't overstate the importance of this type of work. It is something that can draw criticism for on-lookers, they see it as "dance" or "not real enough". But we have to always bear in mind the purpose of the drill. In any case, the concept of "play" is an important one in our training. My friend Bruno Caverna has devoted a lot of time and skill in developing this approach to movement in his Play Fight and Liquid Body school. I recommend you check his work out if this is an area of interest.

At some point this interplay becomes back and forth. A re-directs and throws B, but B feels and responds with a takedown, which A avoids and so on. We now have a dynamic situation in which we can further develop those attributes of sensitivity, centre and direction, as well as our own fluidity of reaction and response. All of these things feed directly back into our "real world" work and also have profound benefits on many other levels. Life can be a series of locks and throws, learn to roll with them.

## WORKING WITH TENSION

Let's next address the issues of tension and resistance next. We know that with a like-minded partner we can develop great awareness and movement. But what happens when a person is resistant to our movements? There are two basic methods, we either work with the tension or we work to re/move it.

Taking the second one first, imagine a scenario where A want to put a wrist lock onto B. B is not happy about this and grabs A's shirt really tight. If A tries to apply the lock direct, it will never work. So A gives B a strike - it might be to the solar plexus. The strikes should have the effect of moving B's tension from the hand to the solar plexus. The body naturally tenses in fear reaction to the hit. As the hand is now more relaxed, A can apply the lock.

This is a basic principle of restraint work but we have to caveat it. First on the basis of reasonable force (depending on the situation and your local laws). A hit into a muscle to relax it is one thing, cracking someone's skull with a baton is something else. Second, we have to understand how to hit a person properly.

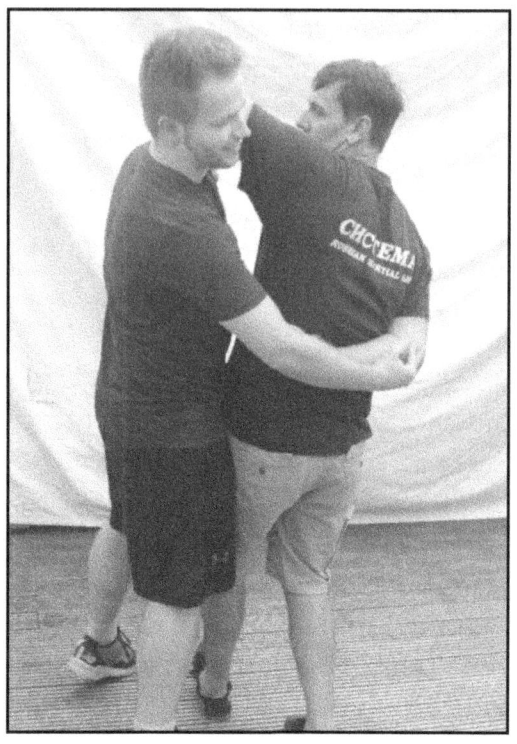

When teaching at other clubs I've often asked people "why do you punch?" Most don't really have an answer other than "that's what we do." In Systema we should always have an awareness of what we are aiming to achieve with a punch and also the ability to vary our delivery of a strike accordingly.

Take the scenario where someone has grabbed you by the collar. Some types of hit will aggravate, Slap the person across the face, for example, and you likely make not only their grip stronger but their response more angry. Drive a knee into the thigh, the classic dead leg, and most people will immediately lurch to that side, as we have removed some support Hit someone correctly in the solar plexus and you strike at the heart of a primal fear - being unable to breathe.

Of course, you can hit a person in such a way to knock them out completely, which may be appropriate in some cases. No-one is more relaxed than when they are asleep!

We can think, then, of one of the definitions of Systema - the collection of body systems that comprise each of us. We have a skeletal, nervous, respiratory, digestive, muscular, immune, endocrine etc system. We also have an emotional / psychological system. When we hit we should be quite specific of which of those we are aiming to influence.

A strike to break a knee primarily effects the bones and therefore the structure. Of course, there will also be nerve signals involved, we are holistic creatures. But a bone strike is usually made to break the structure at its most basic level. Likewise tearing a joint.

A muscle strike can also be made to affect structure, especially where the tension in that muscle is supporting the person in some way - the dead leg earlier being a prime example. It is hard for a person to make a strong grip if the arm muscles are numbed.

The face slap primarily stimulates the nervous system - a large amount of information is suddenly delivered to the brain. In some methods, this can result in overload or neurological shut-down, it is certainly possible to switch a person off with a slap. But the everyday face slap tends to sting, fires up the nervous system and generally stimulate a person.

When we talk about the nervous system people often think of pressure points. We have spoken about those already. In effect, we are asking the nerve to send a fear signal to the brain to either divert the brain's attention or to numb a particular areas. When you bang your funny-bone it's hard to think of anything else and hard to do anything with that hand for a few seconds.

In short, then, apply your hits with a definite idea about what they are doing, don't just flail out and hope for the best. Also be aware of the wider effects of your strike. These may be structural - a hit to the groin usually folds a person forwards, for example. They may also be emotional. It is possible to hit and

frighten a person in such a way that you actually make them more resistant and a better fighter - they may feel they are now fighting for their life. On the other hand, a good well placed strike can drain all the fight out of a person and so allow you to work.

Another fear to use is the fear of falling. ~If someone has grabbed you hard and you sweep their legs or take their balance in some way, the desire to protect themselves while falling usually over-rides everything else. I say usually, because a skilled person may use the fall to develop their attack, as in a sacrifice throw. Also, the fear of falling may make a person hold on to you even stronger! So, as with the hits, taking balance to relax a person needs to be carried out in the right way.

For me, the best way to take the balance is as the person is stepping. We go back to our earlier foot sweep drills. This time, have your partner come in with a grab. Let it just touch, so your partner is committed and time your sweep just as the lead foot places - the hand usually works in conjunction with the feet as people like to feel stable as the grab. The sweep should be a slight movement here, it doesn't take a lot when timed correctly.

Alternatively, what if you have to control a person who is being resistant? If you can get them to take a step, you should be able to put in the sweep and get them to the

floor. But what if you have to move them out of the area and they don't want to go? Resist the temptation to start pushing a person. All this does is create more resistance, no-one likes being pushed about. If you do have to push, work from low down at he base of the spine as we mentioned before. You need to take the whole person with a pull or a push and your movement needs to be focused and assertive.

Fear need not be physical. People fear arrest, they fear looking weak in front of their friends, they fear looking like an idiot and so on. Any work with potentially difficult people needs to take these things into account and we will discuss some further ideas for these scenarios in the next chapter.

So these are some ways to move or remove tension. Let's now look at how we can work with a persons tension. We know that pressure on certain points will cause pain. If a person tenses, that pain doesn't go away, it gets worse, and the person naturally tries to move away from it. Pushing into that tension gives a clear direction in which to move, downward to the floor, for example. If a person is able to relax and move out from under the pressure, the technique will not work.

Another way we can use tension is to push it back into the person's body. As we saw in our earlier chapter with the stick we can push up into the holder's shoulder and lift their centre. A simple technique using this principle is to have A grab B's wrists. The grab should be hard and A puts weight into it. B accepts the grab and gives a slight and sudden movement of the hands towards themselves, ie in the same direction as the grabbing hands are moving. This should bring A in even more and fully load their arms.

B now lifts their hands up and out, keeping the arms slightly rounded. This action should be done not with force from the arms but from the body - think of our wave movement, a slight turn of the hips and a lift. The effect should be to throw A some distance back, it can be quite spectacular when you get it right! One way to approach this is as "lines of tension" in a person's body. Think back to our head tilt method. The pressure applied to the neck creates a line of tension down the spine. As we know, if we push into this the person has to move down. So if you are having difficulty with this concept, visualise the line of tension that your response creates and push along it.

## DENSITY AND SUPPORT

We can also think of tension as density. When a part of the body is tense, it feels "full" to the hand, it has a certain weight or density to it. This density looks for support, either internal or external. In the case of a tense or full fist, it wants to hit a solid object. A person grabbing is looking for something solid to grab. A solid body needs legs or some other base of support to work from. Conventionally, a person applying strength from the upper body will brace the legs in

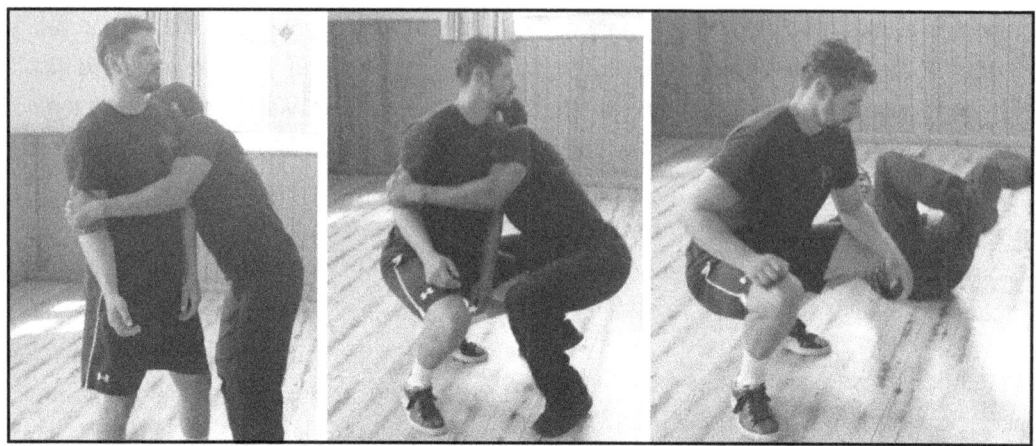

order to reinforce their structure. How can we use this knowledge?

Have A come in with tension and grab B firmly round the shoulders. B tenses the upper body, expanding it to give A full support. If B now quickly relaxes and changes height, A will lose their balance.

Next, A and B take up typical wrestling positions. They lean into each other a little and apply as much force as they can with the upper body. One of the pair suddenly sits or changes position in order to take the support away. This should cause the other partner to stumble and have to re-adjust their posture.

That's the basic principle, let's work to refine it. Next, we add in some direction. A places both hands on B in a strong grab. B should not move to avoid but they should move forward a little, into the grab. This increases the feeling of resistance and support. When you do this work, you really have to feel your partner's weight and tension on you. If you've ever been fishing, think back to that feeling you get when a fish is on the hook. There is a definite pull on the line, you know you have it. If you are struggling to find the feeling, go back to those earlier sensitivity / sticky hand type exercises where you are trying to tap into your opponent's centre.

Simply relaxing may do something but not

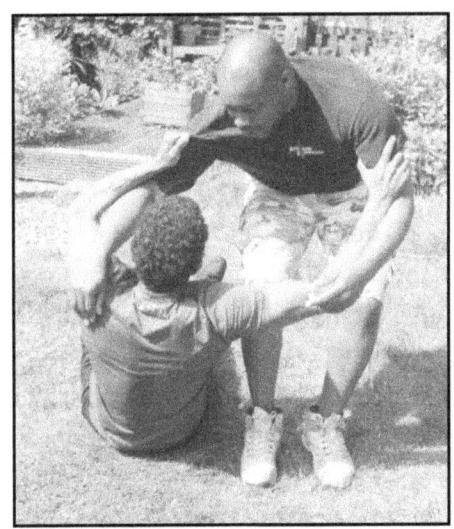

"full" or dense. A leg with no weight on it is empty. In close, we can pull our partner in order to make them step onto one leg, making it dense. We can then attack the full leg with, say, a knee strike or a kick. Driving the knee into an empty leg may have some effect, but not as much as if that leg is firmly planted. An axe works best against a solid tree!

Attacking a full leg means we are working against our partner's internal support. The leg is full because it is holding up the weight of the body. Relaxing the muscles empty the leg will empty and so weaken the structure. The same applies to the body. Hitting into the supporting muscles of the trunk can switch them off and distort structure. To get a feel for this, have your partner grab you and tap into the muscles to relax them. Think of it as a massage!

necessarily enough. So we add in another stage - direction. Having got A "on the hook", B not turns to one side, takes a small step and drops the weight a little. They then quickly relax, removing the support. When done correctly you will be surprised how easy it becomes to throw a person. Once again the sequence is *SUPPORT - DIRECTION - RELAXATION*. Experiment on adding a little wave or spiral into your movement to amplify the effect.

Let's next look at moving our partner's density. A simple way is to think of the legs. When weight is put into a leg, it becomes

We can also work into the density. See how, in the example below, A has come in to grab. B slips out from under the grab and, seeing tension in A's upper back, drives the elbow into that point. As the density in the upper back is unable to dissipate, A will fall. In this

case we can almost think of that density as a weight within the body. From certain angles, the body is unable to carry the weight and will collapse. Again, if the person can release the tension, the method will not work.

**INTERNAL WORK**

Let's now work deeper. All of the methods so far have been quite overt and "external." In other words, the movements are all fairly visible, though, of course, we work to make them more subtle. The phrase "internal work", at least for the purpose of this book, means that much of what is going on is not visible. Use of breath, subtle movements of the body, capturing balance through light touch and so on. In addition there is a very strong psychological element to this work, particularly form the point of view of the person doing it. The mindset must be clam, unhurried, unafraid. With this work we also aim to influence our partner's psyche too, largely through our actions and how we approach the situation.

The challenge in presenting internal work in the written medium is obvious. This level of work is even more feel-based than some of the things we have already covered. A minute adjustment can make all the difference between success and failure. For this reason it is highly advisable to seek out a suitable experienced instructor for guidance. Having said that, there are some simple exercises and drills that we can try to aid our understanding.

We approach this work through the lens of learning and understanding rather than just trying to smash our opponent. We often have to straddle a fine line between making something work and pushing for an outcome. It is best to train with people you know well for this work, people who will give you honest feedback and not work to either "spoil" the drills nor to unquestioningly go along with everything. We must be very scrupulous in our approach and keep the ego in check. Being able to produce results during a drill with a friendly partner does not equate to having super-human abilities.

In my experience, this work has always been presented as mundane, if I can use that term. By this I mean there is nothing supernatural, "chi-powered" or anything else about it. It is simply harnessing a deeper understanding of the human body and psyche.

## INTERNAL STRUCTURE

Let's begin with our own structure. We know from before that using tension can protect a joint, at least in the short term. Our first drill then, is to have A apply the classic wrist lock to B. B accepts the lock but, on contact activates the tendons of the hand. We do this by splaying the fingers out slightly and expanding . Imagine you are stretching the fingers out, reaching out and forward. This should have the effect of reinforcing your internal structure but also feeding in slightly to A's structure. It is very important that A should not feel as though they are being pushed or lifted. The feeling is more as though they are pushing themselves away.

Note how the rest of the body remains relaxed. Its only role is to support the arm / wrist. If you feel any tension creeping in, break the drill, shake yourself a few times and resume. This is building your body's first point of internal support, from wrist to fingers. Once you can do that can experiment with other points of support.

Next A pushes on B's arm in some way. B should feel that they can activate the hand, as before, to reinforce. This time, though, AB activate the pectoral muscle. This means not contracting the muscle but pushing it out a little, as we do in our selective tension exercises. Think of the arm as a stick, we are fixing one end of into a solid support. That support then travels along the arm, so the fingers are projected outwards a little. Again, A should feel as though they are pushing themselves away. Look down, if A's toes are lifting off the ground, it's a good sign! B should check again that the rest of the body is relaxed, particularly that the legs are not braced. The body should be upright too, no leaning - that is just using weight.

The next step is to have A push on the shoulder. Now B activates the spine and hips. No stance, no grounding or leaning. The body is upright, the limbs mobile. But the central core is being maintained, again

there should be that feeling of outward expansion. To A it should feel like pushing on a large tyre or balloon. The surface is soft but there is an inner buoyancy. The challenge for B is also to keep the centre up high in the chest, not to drop into the balance point.

CONNECTING

We use this method to connect into our partner's structure. We should already feel that slight unbalancing effect on contact. So let's take that a little further. It is important first to recognise the difference between touch and connect. It is much the same as the difference between looking and seeing. Have you ever lost something and look everywhere for it? We had it with the TV remote the other day. Simply vanished. We looked all around for ten minutes. Of course it was on the TV unit right in front of us all the time. We were looking but did not see Likewise we often touch with feel. Feel implies a de peer level of contact. Think back to the earlier drill of resting your hands on a partner's shoulders. Be quiet and patient and you begin to feel their internal movement. This is the same, except we are feeling that through the point of contact that they provide.

So now A places their hands on B, any position. B activates their internal support as before, so feeding into A's structure. B now only needs make a slight movement

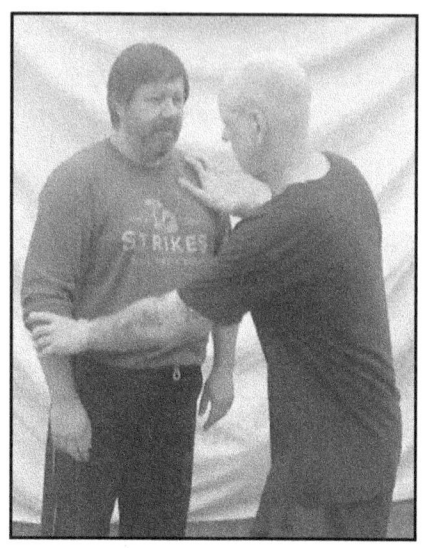

in order to take A's balance. There should be no pushing or pulling as such, no sudden change in direction. In fact the smaller and smoother B's movement is the better. To the casual on-looker the result looks totally out of proportion to the amount of movement and perceived effort involved. This it is why this work has to be felt, it is tactile not visual. The subtlety is part of the reason, I think, for the large reaction. When we know or feel we are

being moved, our body prepares itself. In much the same way that if we see a punch coming, we can brace into it, or prepare to absorb it.

Imagine your are blindfold and taking strikes - in fact, this is a good exercise to do at some point. You have no visual sense of when and where the blow is landing. Your body works on a purely tactical level. Everyone I know at first, including me, flinches really hard at the first touch, even if it is quite light. Over time, we learn to trust our body and let it respond purely as it needs too. I think a similar mechanism is at play here. We grab and feel support under our hands. However, puzzlingly, we find ourselves a little of balance. Before we can response, that support dissolves and we fall into the void created. As our body has had no chance to prepare, their tends to be a big flinch from our muscles, as though everything is tensing to protect our organs. It's also a little like missing a step in the dark, it can send us flying.

In other words we are operating under our partner's radar. No overt movement, just through using that connection. This has deeper implications on a psychological level. We all have psychological "hooks". If a person can contact those in the same way, they can be used to unbalance, control, direct or even destroy is. This is beyond the scope of this book but I would ask you to give it some thought.

Back to the physical. If you are struggling with this concept, or you are looking to refine it further, here are some more drills to try. We work these from a kneeling position.

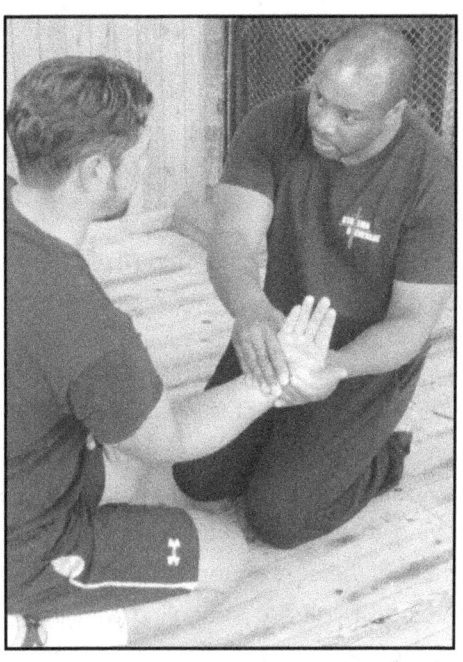

DRAINING TENSION

This time we will use the same principle to drain tension and re-direct or lead it. We start with A grabbing B's wrist as shown. The grip should be strong. On contact, B activates their internal support as before. If you look at the photo above, you will see that A is giving a direction to the movement, away to B's right. B feels and follows this direction but then works to subtly re-direct it.

B continues this re-direction out of A's power arc. If A maintains the strong grip, they will find their whole body following B's redirection. In this case B is also using a light

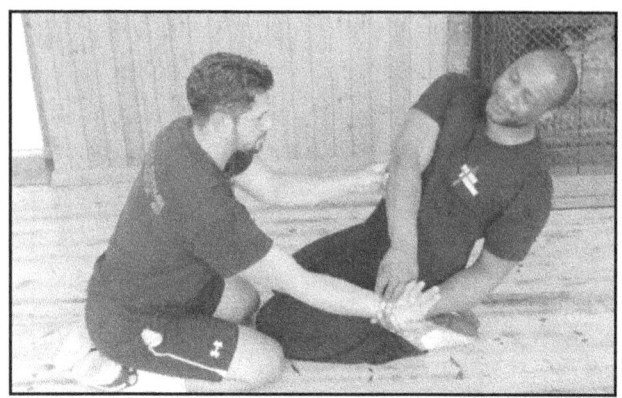

touch from the other hand to reinforce the direction.

The principle here is similar to our *support - direct-relax* concept from earlier but on a more subtle level. A should feel as though they are in control throughout and are moving themselves. There should be no sense of being pushed, pulled or even directed. If you are struggling with this at first, go back to our wave movement. B places their free hand on A's elbow, then uses A's grab to start a wave from the grabbed hand, across the shoulders and out the other hand. The wave should amplify the direction, in effect B is using A's movement to push them away.

Work to shrink this wave down, make it as much of an internal movements as you can. From the outside it should be little more than a light ripple across the shoulders.

The next stage also works from the same set-up. A grabs B's wrist and holds tight. This time B does not move, they just hold their position, but must keep the grabbed hand full. Also, as the grip is applied, B should slightly expand the body. Inhale and raise the chest, for example. A maintains the pressure. B now lightly touches A's elbow, this is to keep A's arm aligned and tense. B now exhales and relaxes the rest of their body as much as possible, while keeping the grabbed hand full. If the chest was expanded, it contracts. Shoulders that were raised can be lowered. The trick is to know just how far to relax. If we relax completely, it allows A access into the internal system. B needs to maintain

next work with the body. A now applies two hands directly on to B. Once again, B inhales and expand slightly on contact. B keeps a little density directly under A's hands, in order to establish that connection we spoke about earlier. B may already feel a direction from A - it is likely that one hand is applying more pressure than the other. B exhales and relaxes in that direction (while maintaining the points of support). Again, there should be no overt movement or turning here. A should feel as though the force of their push is moving slowly out to the side - or wherever it is directed.

structural integrity . It is this act of relaxing that now gives A a direction rather than any overt movement on B's part. As B relaxes they sink down into their posture. If done right, A will feel their strength / tension flow away. It is as though there is nothing to apply it to.

The next stage is to add in some movement. A comes in with a dynamic grab, B works the same principle. Establish a connection, feel the direction, relax into it. Work as slow as you need at first to develop the timing then add in more speed as you go.

Tension thrives on resistance. If B tenses in the above case, A likely applies even more tension. We can actually make our opponent stronger. If we collapse like a rag doll, our opponent has full control. This "in-between" method gives just enough for our partner to latch on too but then subtly removes the support. And this should be subtle, not the big level change or twisting movement of before. It may be that at first you find you need to add in a more overt direction change but you should work to minimise this.

Once you have this feeling in the hands,

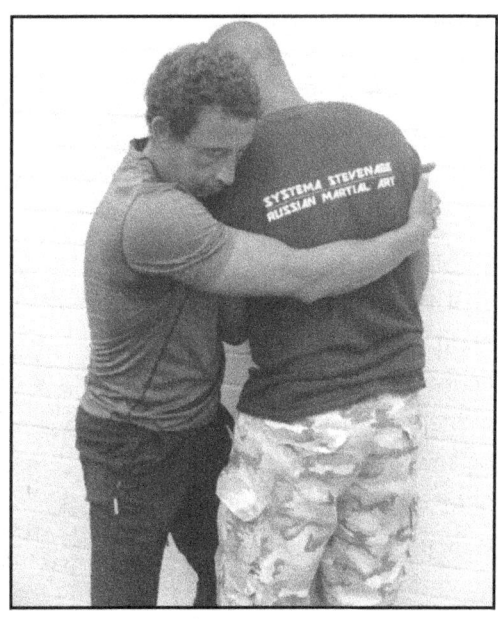

## POWER IN THE HANDS

We mentioned keeping the hands full earlier. This is especially relevant to punching but does have some relevance to our work here too. First, what do we mean by power? People often think of this a strength, as direct muscular tension. Strength is certainly a component of power (though more tendon or applied strength than brute force). But so are position, movement, timing and relaxation.

To get a feel of power in the hands it is good to work with weapons. Holding a sword the correct way brings a certain feeling with it. The hand feels full and ready to work. I've found a good way to develop this feeling is by using a sledgehammer but you could try with a stick, kettlebells or similar. Stand in a natural position and bring the hammer up as shown. The first thing you will feel is how the weight of the head makes the hammer unsteady. In order to keep the hammer still, you have to apply

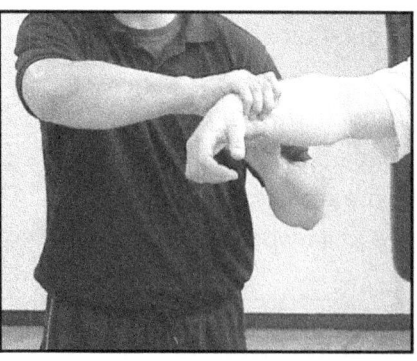

some grip with the hand. But the tension of this grip should not travel up the arm at all, the rest of the body must remain relaxed.

Now move around a little, take a few steps. Feel again how the power in the and maintains the position of the hammer. The grip is a squeezing motion, imagine you are gathering power in the hand. Naturally, you can go back to our grip exercises from the earlier chapter and approach those in the same way. Don't think of applying strength, think of applying power.

Once you have the feeling, work with a a partner. Grab their clothing or grab some part of the body and apply power to the grip. Your partner should feel the difference and you should also find that the rest of your body remains relaxed and does not get so locked in with your hold.

## ACTIVE WORK

The first set of drills we have shown here are all passive, in the sense that we have our partner grab us or apply some lock or hold. But what about when we need to actively engage another person, can these internal principles still be applied? Yes they can and one place to start is with a simple stick drill.

Before, we worked on exercises where one person guides the other's movement via the stick. This time, A and B stand opposite each other, both firmly holding the stick. B first activates the internal structure as before, in order to bring power into the grip. B then uses this to establish a sense of connection with A, via the stick. At first it helps if A is tense.

Of course, B can push or pull with stick from here in order to move A. But we are looking for that more subtle approach. B feels or gives a slight direction to A - and it should be very slight. At first I suggest extending forward a little. Check A's feet, if their toes are slightly raised, then B has the connection. Next, B maintains the connection but relaxes into that direction. A should be moved with no apparent effort from B.

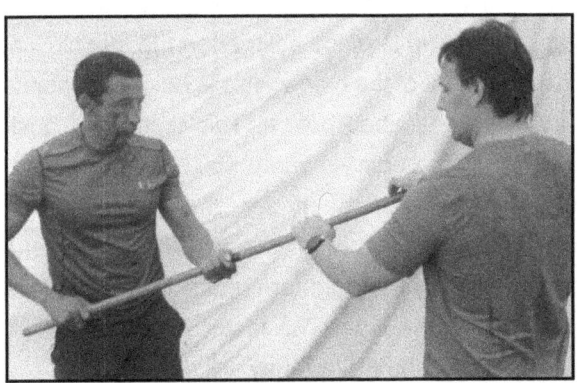

Once you can do this, A and B vary positions and grip. Then add in movement. Start with a simple grip but A and B are walking around. B should now see if they can "switch on" that connection when A is in mid-step. This should make unbalancing even easier. The final step is for A and B to slowly wrestle with the stick. B needs to feel when they should be full and when they should be empty. Think back to that feeling of fullness or power in the hands, feel for the tension that the other person gives you and always be monitoring yourself for unwanted tension, physical or emotional.

When using the stick we are primarily working with or into our partner's arms. Once you have that feeling, begin to

work directly into their body. A walks to B. B places a hand on A and establishes contact. You will probably find that the chest is the easiest place to start. B next rotates the hand in and down slightly. Done correctly, this creates tension in A's chest That tension should be enough to stop their forward movement by brining tension down into the hips and legs. Again we stress this should be as subtle as possible. At first, naturally, you will find you are pushing quite hard in an attempt to get a result. This is fine but try working with the mindset of no result, with less effort and you may be surprised at the results.

Once you can switch on a muscle, try the same drill and switch a muscle off. We know this can be done by striking but try also working from a soft touch. Sometimes a light stroking is enough to relax a muscle, if we move in the right direction Sometimes locking the muscle in place for a second will force it to switch off. Or see how you can transfer your own relaxation into the other person.

The next stage is for B to place the hands on other parts of the body and create some effect with the same method. A can be as active or as passive as you like. The goal for B each time is to establish connection via touch, then use their own internal state to either switch on or switch off a particular muscle in A.

To start getting an idea of how this works in application, have A grab B by the throat. B activates the neck, giving support to A's arm, pushing back into the shoulder a little to slightly tilt A's balance. B next brings their hand up to place a finger on the muscle just in front of the elbow - this is one of the points we described before. This time don't push into the point, though. Make a light upward curve with the finger. If you have good connection through the arm, that movement, with a very slight turn of the waist will move A off the side. The faster A comes in, the faster and further they will go out.

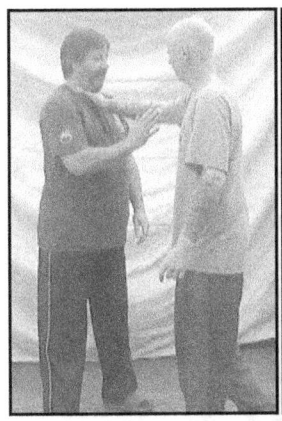 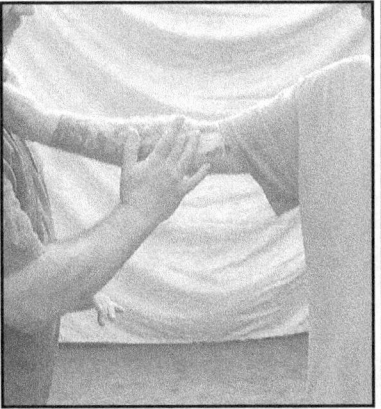 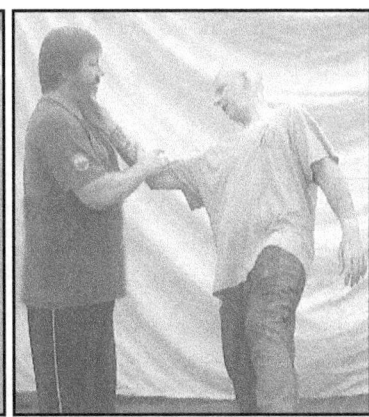

If you run into difficulties, always dial back and return to a simple static exercise to regain the feeling - because this this is all about feeling. While all our principles of triangulation, leverage and so on are at play, we are applying them in a much more subtle way than with the external methods from before. Be patient and don't rush, this is not the sort of work you develop overnight. But if you can learn to work this way, you will find everything becoming much smoother, calmer, more efficient and more effective.

I often say that this type of "soft" work looks much nicer than tension-filled "sharp" work. While it can certainly be used to deal with people in a more humane way, there is also much more potential for damage here too. You should be aware of this when practicing, particularly at speed. As we said before, when the body has no warning of a change or a turn it is unprepared. At slow speed this change can be managed. At high speed, with the inclusion of the fear and tension that comes with it, sudden torqueing of joins or weight being spiraled through different parts of the body can cause severe injury beyond what you may expect from a "gentle" pat on the back. In this respect, for the other person the exercise also becomes a lesson in learning to deal with such sudden changes and forces.

This is one of the great beauties of Systema. Unlike the traditional "attacker-defender" roles, all participants on a drill have an opportunity to learn from the experience, and the deeper the work, the greater the opportunity. This is why so many people queue up at workshops to be hit or thrown by Mikhail. There is a deeper level of communication going on here than may at first be apparent, providing we are receptive to it. So please approach this work in that mindset, as an exploration, as a way of bringing knowledge that already exists in our bodies outwards. Because we are not learning anything new here, this is old knowledge that we are awakening, knowledge that our ancestors used in their day to day work and survival.

## LIGHT AND NO CONTACT WORK

Now we come to one of the most controversial areas of training. This is most often down to misunderstanding. Some like to characterise this work as "magic", student gullibility, "chi power" or other such misrepresentations. The truth is, we all do no contact

work several times a day. Simple body language is the prime example. Next time you are having a chat to someone, suddenly point over their shoulder - 99% they will look round. There, you have mastered no contact work!

Other day to day examples include the pavement dance - when you are headed directly towards someone on the street and you both indicate you are moving aside for

the other person; flinching when a lamppost suddenly pops ups in front of you; smiling back when someone smiles at you; recoiling on your sofa when something nasty flashes up on screen during a horror movie; jumping before your realise that big spider is just a plastic one that your wife put there to scare you (it's all fun and games in our house!). In short, all normal aspects of our regular flinch response, fear mechanisms, social behaviours and so on.

How do we work this into our holds and throws work? Let's start with a basic progression, from heavy to light to no contact. A rushes in to B and grabs them with both hands. B allows the grab to bite, goes with the movement, takes a step, grips A in some way and throws them in the direction they were going. Repeat a few times.

A rushes in to grab again. B works earlier. The grab barely touches and B is already moving inside it. B pivots, removing support and directs with a light touch on some part of A's arm of body. A should again be thrown

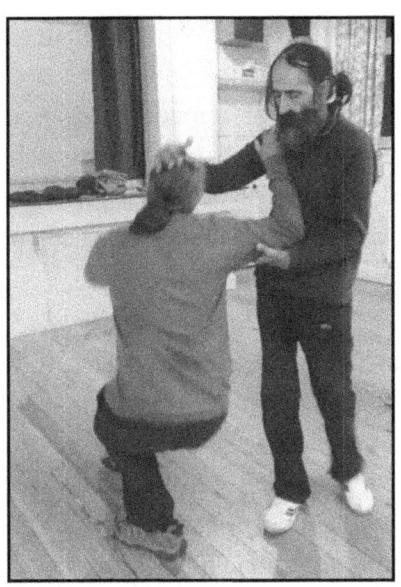

clear. Repeat a few times. Run the same drill again. This time B tries to use even lighter contact. Then go for no contact.

A rushes in. As they get close B very obviously pushes one shoulder forward, then dips it out of the way and can also change level. This causes A to adjust, then adjust again as they are stepping. If they are going quite fast, the resultant change can cause A to lose balance. In effect, they throw themselves.

This is the basic principle for this type of no contact work. As you can see, we are primarily playing with the method of support, from a visual perspective. Actually, I would say that all of this type of no contact work is from a visual perspective. We are sending a signal to the other person's brain that over-rides and disrupts in some way their intended movement. There are two aspects to this, leading and interrupting

## LEADING

We speak at more length about this in the *Systema Awareness* book as it is a staple non-physical method for dealing with people who you need to move. It works around that simple "point and look" principle and the idea that where mental focus goes, tension tends to follow. A difficulty when working drills like this is when both partners know what is going to happen! So it may be that you only tell one person what the actual drill is, tell the other "go and grab him." Having said that, these reactions are so ingrained that even when you know it's going to happen, it often still does!

A approaches B with a fast grab. At a certain distance, B looks down, points to the floor between them, and firmly asks "Look! What's that?" A will likely falter in their movement. The head and gaze goes down, the "forward" signal from the brain is interrupted. This buys B a little time in which to work an appropriate response - escape, take action, etc.

Repeat the drill. This time, B holds one arm up as though "welcoming" A in , while the other directs them to the side, giving a clear indication of the direction they should go on.

A third method is, as A draws close, For B to smile and extend an arm out for a handshake. You'd be surprised how many people react by returning it. B can then work into the handshake methods from earlier.

The last one for now is the "over the shoulder" gaze. As A draws near, B looks over their shoulder and nods towards A, you want to give a "there he is, get him!" impression.

There might sound a bit silly and way too obvious to work. These are the most overt and simple methods but it is surprising how effective they are - remember, in the real life the other person doesn't know what you are going to do! There are caveats, of course. A person not in their right mind may not be capable of reading such signals, likewise a person with extreme bad intentions towards you. But in things like door situations or lower lever risk scenarios they are a useful addition to the tool box.

There is one last method here that works perfectly if a person is drunk, though. Difficult to simulate in training but this is the set up. A (drunk) is arguing with B. B makes eye contact and talks calmly back. As they do so they walk in a slow circle around A. In other words, A has to turn constantly in order to keep up, adding to the general disorientation that a good load of drink brings. I've heard of people actually stumbling and falling over through this, which then makes the door staff's job much easier.

INTERRUPTION

With this principle we are looking to cut a person's movement short rather than re-direct. Of course, both principles can be worked together, but if we want an initial halt, there are a couple of ways to achieve it. The first is through sound and vision.

A rushes to B as before. As A gets close, B holds up a palm and gives the order "Stop!."
This may make A halt, especially if they are person used to taking orders (aka being married).

I once read of this method being used successful by a middle aged lady being hassled on a tube train in London. She went into full "English nanny" mode, "Stop that immediately, What on Earth do you think you are doing!" and the person did! Obviously this is very much a method that relies on aspects of our upbringing and social conditioning. Perhaps a person who has been in the army will respond to a barked, Sergeant Major type order. Or it may be a more paternal or maternal feelings in the case above. So this approach needs to be selected with care and, importantly, needs to be delivered with authority and without fear.

Don't think it has to be loud, though. As an experiment I once asked a student to attack me in some way and not stop whatever I said. As he came in, I quietly said "Oh, hang on a minute," and, of course, he stopped. This obviously plays on an instructor - student dynamic and I'm not saying this is a verbatim technique to use "on the street". But it is a principle to consider. There may be a situation where you need to calm the other person and bellowing at them will not do that. Mikhail once said of this type of work, "Imagine the other person is a child. You have to soothe them, help them go to sleep." As always, context is king.

The second interrupt uses fear. We have to first understand where fear "lives" in the body. There are seven main locations - knees, groin, solar plexus, heart, throat, eyes, base of skull. Generally, a perceived strong threat towards on of these areas will elicit a flinch response. For more information on how fear effects our system, I refer you again to Systema Awareness. In short, the body reacts to a threat by moving away from it, or at least by stopping movement towards it. This is how our bodies work on a cellular lever. Cells only have two movements - towards nutrients, away from danger.

This is simple to try out. A rushes to B again. As they draw close, B puts out a clear and firm move towards A's eyes. A's body stops and bends back a little but the legs continue forward. Experiment with each of the areas and see what response you get - again with the caveats of A not knowing what you are going to do. B should also exercise good control. In reality, if the person keeps moving the kick or strike lands, of course. Watch for how that fear creates tension and density in

your partner. You may not even need physical contact to then control that density. This method combined both interruption and leading. Have partner A rush in fast. As they get close, partner B lifts a hand suddenly up towards A's eyes. Done well, this will bring A's density up into the upper body and "hook" A in.

We spoke before about a deeper physical connection with the hand, this time we are establishing a very strong visual / emotional connection. A has stopped out of fear. That fear has created a ball of tension. What B now has to do is direct that tension. It's almost like someone waiting for direction as to where to go. We run this a lot in close protection drills - it is surprisingly easy to deflect a person's direction of travel by giving them a clear indication of where they should be going.

The same applies with this type of density, if you have the right connection. So B now sweeps the hand in a particular direction A's density will naturally follow that movement, taking A's whole body with them. Done properly, this might look like some kind of magic or trickery to some but it is a simple, everyday principle put to a different use.

These types of drills can be easy to "spoil." In the early days, I was demonstrating the use of a movement towards the eyes to make someone stop. I showed it a couple of times, all went well. One guy insisted on trying it for himself. He walked slowly in, I put out my fingers and he continued slowly walking until my fingertips were literally resting on his eyelids. Great. He "beat" the drill. He missed the opportunity to learn anything from it but he won. Balance was later restored when we started to work on strikes.

**WORKING INSIDE MOVEMENT**

I've mentioned this a few times throughout the book so will explain what I mean by it. There are two obvious positions we can be when some attacks us. Inside or outside of their fight arc. This is the zone created when both arms are raised up in from of person. This is where they will be at their strongest and, usually, most aware.

For some types of striking work, or for evasion, it is good to slip off to the side, away from this arc. We can then be said to be working outside our partner's movement.

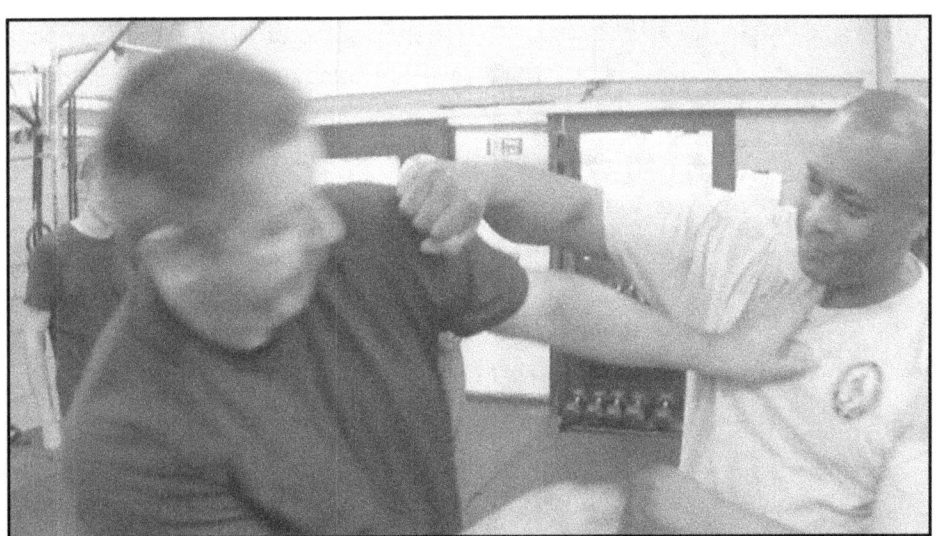

If we remain within the fighting arc, we are working inside our partner's movement. This is a double edged sword - on the one hand we are much closer to our partner's core and it is a target rich environment! On the other hand, the same also applies to our opponent.

We also have to consider that to move forward into a fast, aggressive attack, takes a certain mindset. We come back to our principles of calmness, a professional approach and so on. It also means that we are generally more open in our work. Systema people rarely hunch over and cover up as we see in some methods. This is fine in a sports setting, where certain targets are prohibited, so can protect the head without having to worry about the knees, for example.

In other settings, it is impossible to protect everything. Our best defences are awareness and movement, picking up our attacker's intent earlier and moving with or against it. If we crouch over huddle up we compromise not only our mobility but our awareness. We become a bunker rather than a tank! Working inside doesn't mean that we don;t evade. But we do so by adjusting our frame rather than taking big steps. As we have seen in earlier drills, sometimes a simple roll of the shoulders is enough to misalign a person's grab.

But this is not just physical work, it is also psychological. I have written elsewhere about the OODA Loop, or there are plenty of places to research it on-line. In short, we also work inside our opponent's mind. We can learn to manage their attention, to interrupt their usual thought process to break up and confuse their fixed action patterns.

For holds and restraint work this is doubly important as, by its very nature, we are forced into working up close and personal with people. And, as any professional will tell

you, half the battle is psychological. If you can get compliance by verbal means, the rest of the work is easy.

So work on your timing as an important part of your overall method. I have described this before as the three ranges. In martial arts people often define these as kicking, punching and grappling range - the physical distances involved are quite obvious. I prefer to think in time:

- something is going to happen
- something is happening
- something has happened

Applied to someone grabbing us, this means the person has decided to grab and is positioning themselves; the grab is reaching for us: the person has grabbed us. Generally, we want to be responding as soon as possible. However, as we have seen in some of our methods, on occasion we are happy to work a little later, as our attacker has committed to their course of action. We can use their position or their movement against them.

But what we want to happen is not always what actually happens! So we must learn to be comfortable at ll of those "ranges." As we have seen with some of the previous work, we learn to counter at all stages of a grab, lock, or throw. This also means learning to respond rather than react. If we are taken by surprise there is a good chance our nervous system will spike and initiate a flinch or freeze reaction. Initially, our training can help us overcome that freeze and turn a flinch into a response. As we progress, we can learn to flow directly into a response, often by-passing the flinch stage totally.

This is also a two way process. We may have to initiate work against another person. In this case we still go through the same range process. This is where we have to strike a fine balance between having a plan and being adaptable to change on the move. Our shoulder grab may have to change to a waist grab halfway through. This is where our understanding of principle over technique really comes into play. Technique is very specific. It requires a very particular set of requirements, angles, position and so on. If one thing is even slightly out, it can throw the technique off. Principle is universal. A lever is a lever, whether it's a finger, an arm or a six foot pole.

## PRECISION

If I had to sum up all of our previous chapters' work in one word it would be this - precision. Take any activity or endeavour that requires skill - spots, music, art, carpentry, any sort of craft. The expert or master exhibits precision in all cases. From how a person picks up and holds a brush to the delicate lines or broad strokes they paint. From how someone holds a violin to the emotion they can express through their touch on the strings. A marksman who can remain calm under pressure and hit a distant target despite a strong cross-wind.

Very different activities yet each person exhibits very similar qualities, a combination of awareness, sensitivity, applied strength or power, structure, judgement and so on. It is this combination that gives rise to precision.

When watching newer people work I sometimes see that they go to grab an elbow but do not quite get it - they grab just above or below it. They may also have an awkward grip, the hand is turned around, their own forearm is twisted. There can be many reasons for this, though they are usually related to physical or emotional tension. This is one reason for starting slow and comfortable in the skill acquisition phase of training - it encourages us to be precise. Think of all the attributes you develop as being their to support this precision. Once you have an element of precision you can begin to test it. Work up to a level where precision begins to break down, then dial back a little.

Feel and touch is a major part of this work, but I've also found a visual aid that has helped me too - and that is the idea of shapes. The human body is limited to certain patterns of movement or shapes. So if I see an arm in a certain shape., I know that the elbow will be easily moved in a particular direction. Or take the overall shape of a person as a whole - where is their tension? Is their posture slightly out of line? Read people in the way an outdoor person reads the weather. Learn to recognise these shapes, both visually and by touch and you will find your work that much easier to apply.

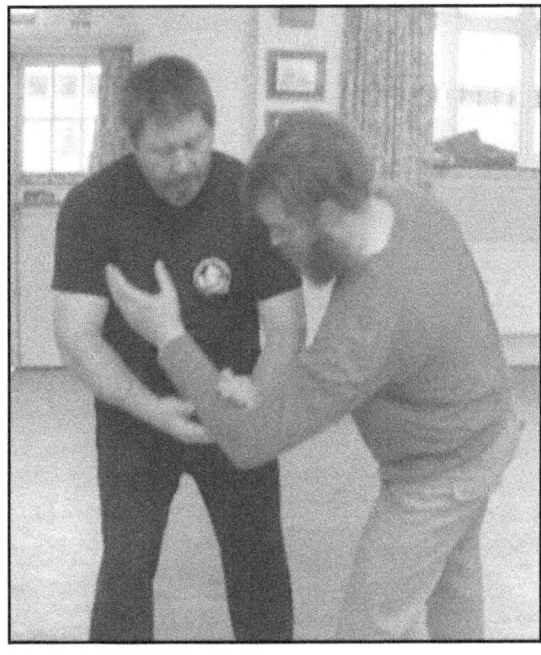

# CHAPTER TWELVE
# DRILLS

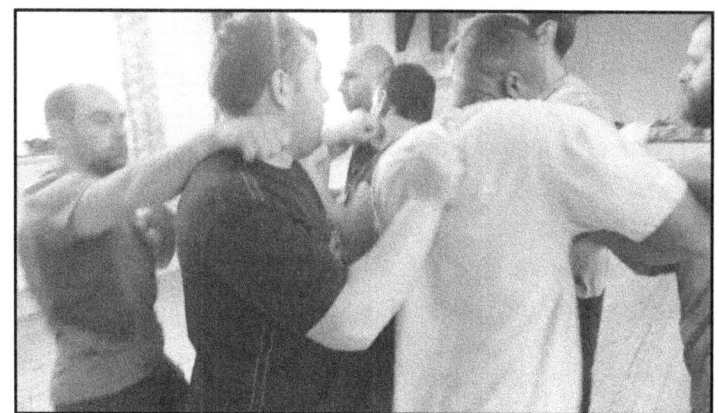

We will finish the book with a look at some ideas for training drills and ways to develop our skills and attributes. Again, we could take a technique approach to this. I could describe dozens of drills, each with its own particular nuance. Instead, I want you to think about the principles of how drills are created and of the variables that you can tweak within them

I cover these ideas in more detail in *The Ten Points of Sparring* but will briefly run through them here, with an eye to the type of work we have been covering. I'll also add in some specific drill and scenario ideas that you can use as templates or as a starting point for developing your own. So let's first think of al the variables we have in training. I came up with these ten before, you may be able to think of more. They arc:

**PURPOSE**

Presumably we are training for a purpose. That is not to say we do not occasionally work just for the pleasure of it but, even then, there is some framework in place. So consider first what you want people to get from the drill. It could be any of these

ATTRIBUTES - awareness, movement, sensitivity, balance, mindset, flow, etc

SKILL ACQUISITION - applying a particular lock, partner work, using a stick, etc

TESTING - sparring, working under pressure, scenarios, problem solving, etc

PLAY - for developing flow, free movement, a chance to try new ideas out, etc

Once you have that idea in place, it is easy to design the drill. There can be cross-over, of course. Developing a skill will naturally develop attributes alongside it. However I would say that Skill Acquisition and Testing do not mix. I can think of few, if any, endeavours, where skill acquisition is carried out under pressure. Imagine your first driving lesson being at Spaghetti Junction in rush hour, right?

The next thing is to establish the method. Let us say the purpose is to learn how to apply the basic gooseneck wrist lock. What do we need? Well, a partner is a good start! So, this will be a pair drill. Next, the partner's need to be working in close and A needs to give B access to their wrist. It might sound glaringly obvious to say this but, as I may have mentioned before, I have actually seen this set up, where A then tucks their hands under their arms and runs around the room. Great if we are doing a chase drill!

So sometimes you have to remind people of this - in fact if I had a school this would probably be up on a sign somewhere:

*THE PURPOSE OF THE DRILL IS NOT TO DEFEAT THE PURPOSE OF THE DRILL*

Every rule has an exception and I would say in the case of some types of scenario training or operational exercise, people should be encouraged to be creative and think outside the box. For stock, standard, development drills, though, it's best to stick with the program.

## SPEED

Think speed of explanation at first. As an Instructor to do dash off a quick wrist lock and say "there yo go?" Or do you drone on for 40 minutes about angle and planes, that time you saw this guy get locked at a wedding, how this relates to the price of beef, etc etc? I have been on the receiving end of both those in previous arts. One, a teacher who seemed bored to be showing such basic stuff, and the other a "combatives" instructor who spent most of the day regaling us with "war stories" about how he'd "effin' effed people up in various effin' tough biker bars" using his "groundbreaking" method.

So, keep instructions clear, brief and on point. I usually give a quick verbal explanation, then demonstrate a few times. If someone asks to feel, I apply the lock to them. Then let the people go away and practice. Stop talking, observe and correct when necessary. Another issue is the instructor who shows one thing, people are halfway through doing it and he or she is already into showing something else. Give people a chance to learn. Likewise, you

don't have to do that one thing for an hour, generally speaking.

The next context of speed is in applying the work. Naturally, slow for learning, faster for development and testing. For locks and holds work you will find it is naturally slow at first as it is less "twitchy" than strike based or knife work can be.

## DISTANCE

This is fairly set for most of our lock and throw drills, in that the work has to be carried out close in. However that is not to say you can't have drills where people have to close the gap and apply a hold, or where one person is trying to escape. For a basic skill drill, though, we need to be in close.

## CONTACT

In context of holds, we are almost always working with contact, so this is less of a variable than striking work.

## TECHNIQUE

Is the work limited to one particular technique or target area? Our earlier example was the gooseneck. Do we stick with this or, once people have grasped the principle, do we allow people to vary the technique? Or we might just say "work to lock the wrists" and give people freedom to explore options.

## COMPLIANCE

How much resistance should our partner's give us? Again, it depends on the purpose of the drill and there are also safety considerations. When it comes to locks, people often equate resistance with tension. This can be useful to explore but we also have to bear in mind the risk of injury. I learned a salutary lesson many years ago when a friend of mine "challenged" a teacher who was applying locks. Everyone else was happy to feel the lock applied, they understood it was a learning experience. My friend went fully tense and tried to strong his way out of it. The instructor made a sudden twist and change in direction and the lock went on fully on, with a crunch. My friend had his wrist in plaster for a while. So understand that in some martial traditions, resistance can be seen as a challenge and that challenge may be answered.

There is a time and a place for resistance. But make it intelligent. Once the skill is there, test it by having your partner trying to escape, counter or otherwise resist your locks. This will be more likely in the testing phase.

If you want to apply resistance it is courtesy to ask your partner first. Likewise, if you want to add in strikes or any other element that is not in the original drill. We come back to our school motto again about drill purpose again.

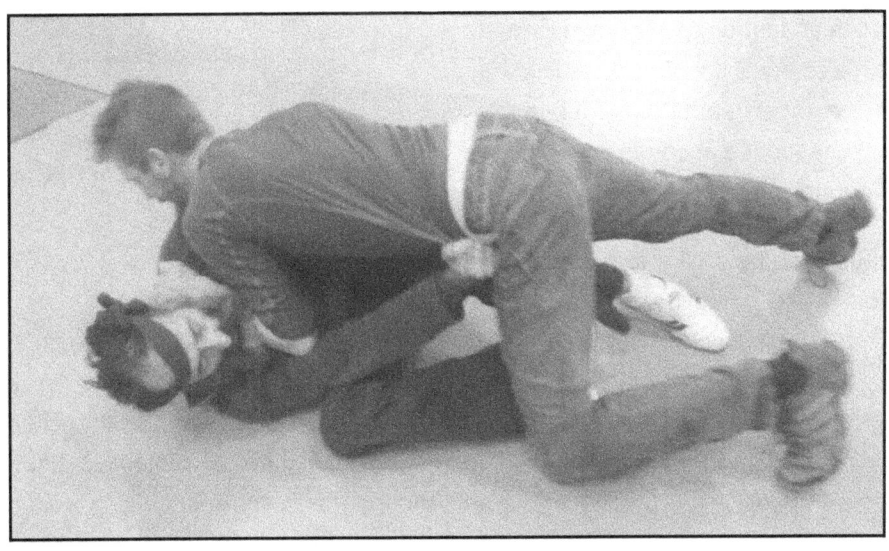

Or I can escape the wrist hold by punching you in the face. I win!

A colleague of mine describes this as "asking a question." In some ways a person can be asking "does this really work" by applying some form of out of context resistance. It can also be down to fear or nerves. As an Instructor it is down to us to ensure the safety of the people training with us, so we must learn to modulate our answer or response accordingly. Anything else is ego taking over.

We should also be aware that sometimes what looks like compliance is a person defending themselves. If you need to roll out of a lock, you roll out of it. If a stick is coming towards you, move out of the way (unless it is a drill to take strikes!). Again, Systema is about all the participants in a drill developing, not being a crash test dummy. If you have to accept the lock full on, treat it as a chance to practice pain management.

## ENVIRONMENT

I would imagine that 99% of martial arts training takes place in tailor made halls, dojos, gyms and so on. From the Systema perspective, the world is our gym. Practice indoors, outdoors, in cars, halfway up the stairs, anywhere you can. We might also think of people in the environment. Why work in pairs all the time? Work threes, fives, whole groups. Each environment has its own challenges and opportunities. And remember if it ain't raining, it ain't training!

## RESTRICTION

This may be in the form of a rule "you can only use one hand," for example. Or it may be something more physical, such as another person holding you while you work. A blindfold is another restriction and a great one for refining and developing our tactile awareness. We can also think of time restrictions, particularly in our sparring drills. A person has a set time limit in which to achieve a particular task.

## EQUIPMENT

We spoke about this in the earlier chapter but, in general, get used to working in different clothes and with different items. We might also think of protective equipment, though this is more for striking work.

## INTENSITY

This is where we blend all our variables together. In musical terms, this is our mixing desk. Or, if you are of a certain age, think of it as a graphic equaliser. Each variable can be set from 1 to 10. So we may set speed at 8 , almost full speed, but keep contact at 2 for a striking drill. Resistance might start at 3 and gradually be increased.

This approach allows us to bring so much variation into our practice. I'm sure those of you who have trained with the main teachers will have experienced and understand this. If you are an instructor look how you can develop this in your own classes. Start with a simple exercise and being tweaking all the variations, you will fill the whole session easily.

## TRAINING DRILLS

I'll give a few ideas here for some specific drills. Again, use these are start points for your own work. Some are for skills or attributes, I'll also add some sparring and scenario exercises. I won't explain too much about what the drills are for, it should be fairly obvious. Besides which , I don't want to pigeonhole too much, sometimes other people find a purpose in drills that I never though of! As always, safety first, learn to walk that line between challenging and dangerous.

## MOVEMENT DRILLS

A lies on their back on the floor with a stick under them. B's job is to try and grab the stick in some way. A moves to try and keep the stick covered.

A lays on their back, B above them. Each holds one end of the stick. B has to try and hit A with the stick in some way. A uses their grip and movement to deflect / escape the hit.

Grab and escape. Working A to B, reverse, then both working. Also try in a group.

A is on the floor, B pins one part of their body - say a hand. A explores how much movement they have from this position.

Two rows face each other about six feet apart. A has to move down the middle of the

Two partners must restrain, pin and then transport another person. Start by emphasising planning and communication. Progress to more resistance from the person.

A has a stick. B applies a grab or hold. See how A can use the stick to escape and restrain B. Vary start positions - both start with hands on the stick, the stick is on the floor between them and so on.

rows, avoiding grabs. Tweak by changing distance, speed, frequent of grabs, etc

Partners work from different positions and in different places. One may be setting down, working in a corridor, on stairs and so on

## ATTRIBUTE DRILLS

## TASK BASED / TESTING DRILLS

A moves towards B, who must place one or both hands on particular parts of A's body. Start with something simple - right hand to left chest, say. Gradually work to cup elbow in palm, touch knee with foot, place fingertips on eyes and so on.

A and B must stand up grapple of 60 seconds and see if they can lock or throw the other.

A has thirty seconds to get B through a doorway. Add in C as a friend of either A or B

A is blindfolded. B slowly comes in and applies a lock or hold. B must escape. Add in extra attackers for more pressure.

A has thirty seconds to pin B to the floor and

## SKILL ACQUISITION

A is locked up by B and C. They allow the locks to come fully on then must find a way to escape.

Have a range of objects to hand - belt, chair, book, etc. Partners must find at least three ways to use each item for restrain or for escaping.

hold them there for another ten seconds.

A and B are door staff. They have to prevent C entering the doorway for sixty seconds. . Add in other bodies on either side as before.

A allows themselves to be pinned by one or two others, then has a minute to get free.

## SCENARIO WORK

These are like task based drills but with a little more of a script. People can play drunk, aggressive, passive or other people in order to add an emotional content into the drill. You can give people specific instructions, such as "I want you to go in and be verbally very aggressive but do nothing physical" for example. Be sure everyone knows their role and have a very clear signal for start and end (a whistle works well). We also put safe words in play should anyone wish to exit the exercise.

Scenarios are run for longer than testing drills in order to allow situations to develop - anything from five minutes up to a few hours in some of our grander exercises!

A is being a nuisance in a club. He is with some friends. B and C are the door staff who have to control the situation.

A has been ejected from the club but is trying to get back in to get his jacket. B and C are the long suffering door staff again.

A is drunk at a family event. B has to remove him safely form the situation.

A cut in front of B in traffic. At the lights, B jumps out and approaches A who is still sitting in their car.

A large fight is going on, A and B arrive and have to restrain the ringleaders.

# CHAPTER THIRTEEN
# CONCLUSIONS

So there we have our guide to Systema locks, holds and throws. I hope you find the book useful. As I said at the start, to produce a technique-based manual on every conceivable position, hold, take down and so on would be nigh on impossible. Instead, through using some basic techniques, I hope I have illustrated the underlying principles that go into making any technique work. In fact, it is better, when you are ready, to stop thinking about technique altogether and just let your body react and respond in the most appropriate way.

This topic is one that is difficult, if not impossible to practice solo. You can, and should, do these and many of the other preparation exercises but, ultimately, this work is based very much on the feel and response of another human body. As I write, we are still in covid lock down, so how this will effect our training long-term is difficult to say. However, even if you can grab a family member (or have them grab you!) you can being working on some things. If solo, then try putting restrictions upon yourself and moving around - this at least gets your body used to moving with less freedom and finding different ways to use your posture and structure.

If you are in a group or are an instructor, then, naturally, this work should be balanced out with all the other topics Systema can cover. It is true to say, to an extent, that attributes and principles are

transferable across a range of activities and situations. While in training we often break things into smaller chunks out for ease of learning, if the situation calls there is no reason not to grab, kick, punch, use a stick, climb a wall to escape or any other thing we need to do.

Before we finish, I'd just like to quickly list the major principles here again, with a few ideas of each, as a quick reference guide for you. Again, the realty is we will be using two or more of these simultaneously, so never think you just have to stick to one method. Be creative, be adaptive, be fluid, most of all, be human.

BREATHING - for control of psyche, for power, for pain management, for movement

COMMUNICATION - verbal engagement, dealing with aggression, partner work

FLOW - smooth transition of position, height, technique and mental outlook

MECHANICS - lever, wheel, cog, etc

MOVEMENT - rotation, spiral, footwork, use of mass

PAIN COMPLIANCE - nerve points, muscle pinching, vulnerable areas

POSITION - angle of take down, placement of feet

PSYCHOLOGY - creating fear, draining will to fight, professional mindset

RELAXATION - switching off muscles, in self for freedom of movement

SENSITIVITY - tactile awareness, pre-emptying movement, emotions, etc

SITUATIONAL AWARENESS - immediate surroundings, use of environment, possible consequences, knowledge of the law

STRUCTURE - disrupting others, maintaining own

TENSION - using tension or density, reinforcing own structure

If you have trouble remembering all those, just think of the useful acronym *BCFMMPPPPRSSST*. Okay, perhaps that isn't much help. Maybe just practice more?

At some stage you must begin to refine your work. That may be on a more external level or it may be on a deeper, internal level. We spoke about precision earlier, try to incorporate that into your practice as soon as possible. You should be mindful of it in all your training, solo and with others. Once you can do takedowns and throws reasonably well, try doing them with less force. See if you can use just finger pressure to collapse structure - it is entirely possible to do so if your placement and angles are correct.

You should eventually find your hands, fist, feet all going to the correct spots in any interaction with another person. You should also find your body moving of its own accord in threatening circumstances - learn to trust your instincts and intuition, another important area of Systema training.

In this respect, although we often separate things out in training, Systema is a comprehensive, cohesive, holistic art, in every aspect. Take massage and manipulation as an example. The knowledge gained by the hands when working massage is also of use when we come to apply our locks and holds - and vice versa. Everything affects everything else!

Unity and calmness in ourselves will influence the people around us. In that sense, Systema becomes a tool for unity in a wider sense. Every single person on the planet experiences the same fears, undergoes the same trials and tribulations, some more acutely than others. If we become finely attuned and sensitive to our own tensions and emotional issues, how can we fail to be aware of those of others? And being aware, how can we not offer some support, advice or assistance?

Looking back over this book, we have covered quite a range of techniques and principles. However there are still many things I feel are left out. Rolling to escape from holds, for example, or even more aspects of internal work. However I hope you find enough here to either give you a guide in beginning Systema training, incorporating some ideas into your own art or style, or bringing some fresh ideas to your existing Systema training. Above all, be creative and adaptive in your training, then take time to analyse results and adjust

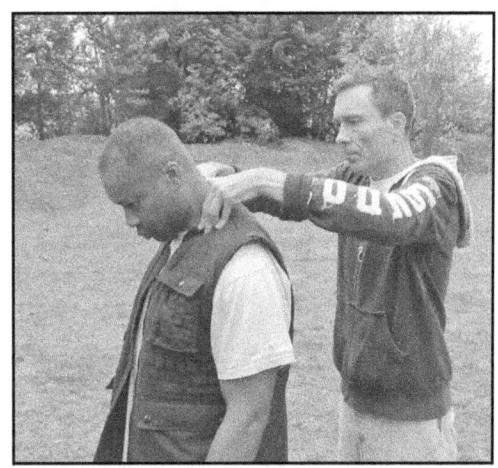

accordingly. It is important to understand that Systema is a process, not a destination. I've been training in it for around 20 years now and feel I am just beginning to scratch the surface. As I change, so does my Systema. There is always something new to discover, whether it be a new drill, a different way to work or a more efficient and relaxed way to carry out a certain task. Give yourself over to the process and Systema will be a precious asset for your whole life.

In conclusion, I'd like to thank my teachers Mikhail and Vladimir again, along with all the other great people I've trained under. I'd also like to thank my friends and students for their continued support, particularly those who helped by posing for the numerous photos in this book. If you have any questions, suggestions or any other feedback then please drop me a line and I'll do my best to respond.

Stay healthy, stay safe and Happy Training!

## RESOURCES

Mikhail Ryabko
Systema HQ Moscow  www.systemaryabko.com

Vladimir Vasiliev
Systema HQ Toronto  www.russianmartialart.com

Cutting Edge Systema  www.systemauk.com

Books & Instructional films  www.systemafilms.com

## RECOMMENDED READING

Strikes - Vladimir Vasiliev & Scott Meredith

Let Every Breath - Vladimir Vasiliev

Secrets of the Russian Blade Masters - Vladimir Vasiliev

The Systema Manual - Major Konstantin Komarov

Other books by Robert Poyton

The Ten Points of Sparring
Systema Solo Training
Systema Partner Training
Systema Awareness Training
Systema Voices
Fitness Over 40
Don't Worry - A Guide to Stress Management
The Eight Brocades

www.ingramcontent.com/pod-product-compliance
Lightning Source LLC
Chambersburg PA
CBHW081109080526
44587CB00021B/3508